I0485699

WISDOM

Proverbs in Coloring Frames
Lovink Coloring Books

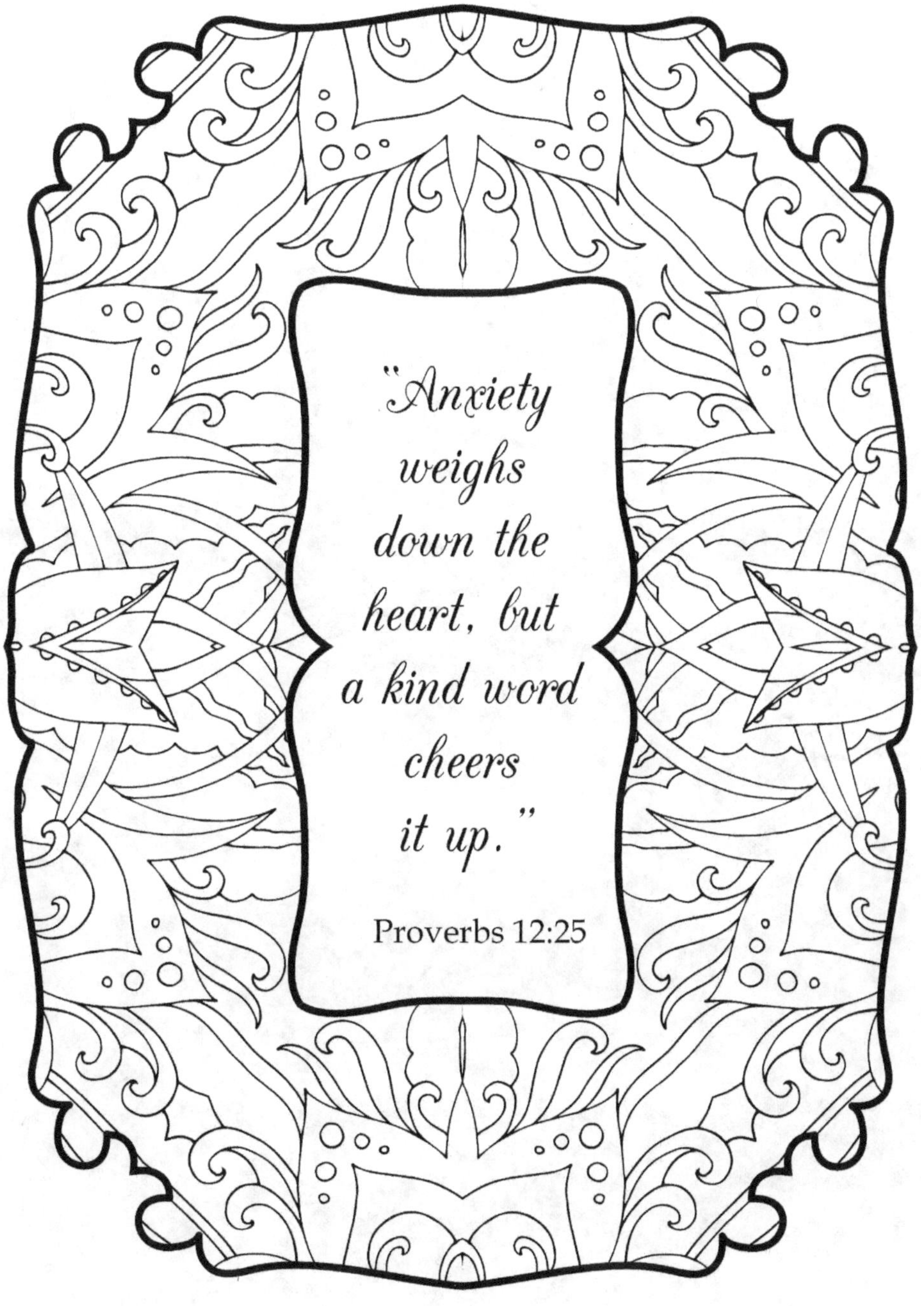

"Anxiety weighs down the heart, but a kind word cheers it up."

Proverbs 12:25

Joan Smith

Copyright © 2015 Lovink Coloring Books

All rights reserved

Steps to a Relaxing Coloring

As an adult, you can enjoy coloring just as much as you did as a child. To make it a *truly relaxing experience*, try following these steps:

1. Find a quiet space. It's easier to focus on what you are doing when there are no distraction.

2. Organize your materials. Lay out your coloring book and crayons or pens.

3. Set the mood. Turn on some tranquil music, diffuse lavender or another relaxing oil and make sure you have your preferred drink at hand.

4. Select your picture. Which image speaks to you today? That's the one you should color.

5. Choose your palette. Select the colors you will be using for your image.

6. Begin coloring. This is the fun part. Don't worry about getting everything perfect, just start.

Allow yourself to relax and focus on the coloring. You'll find it is an amazing way to alleviate stress and take a little time out from the day's hassles. If you feel don't want to do it anymore, just stop!

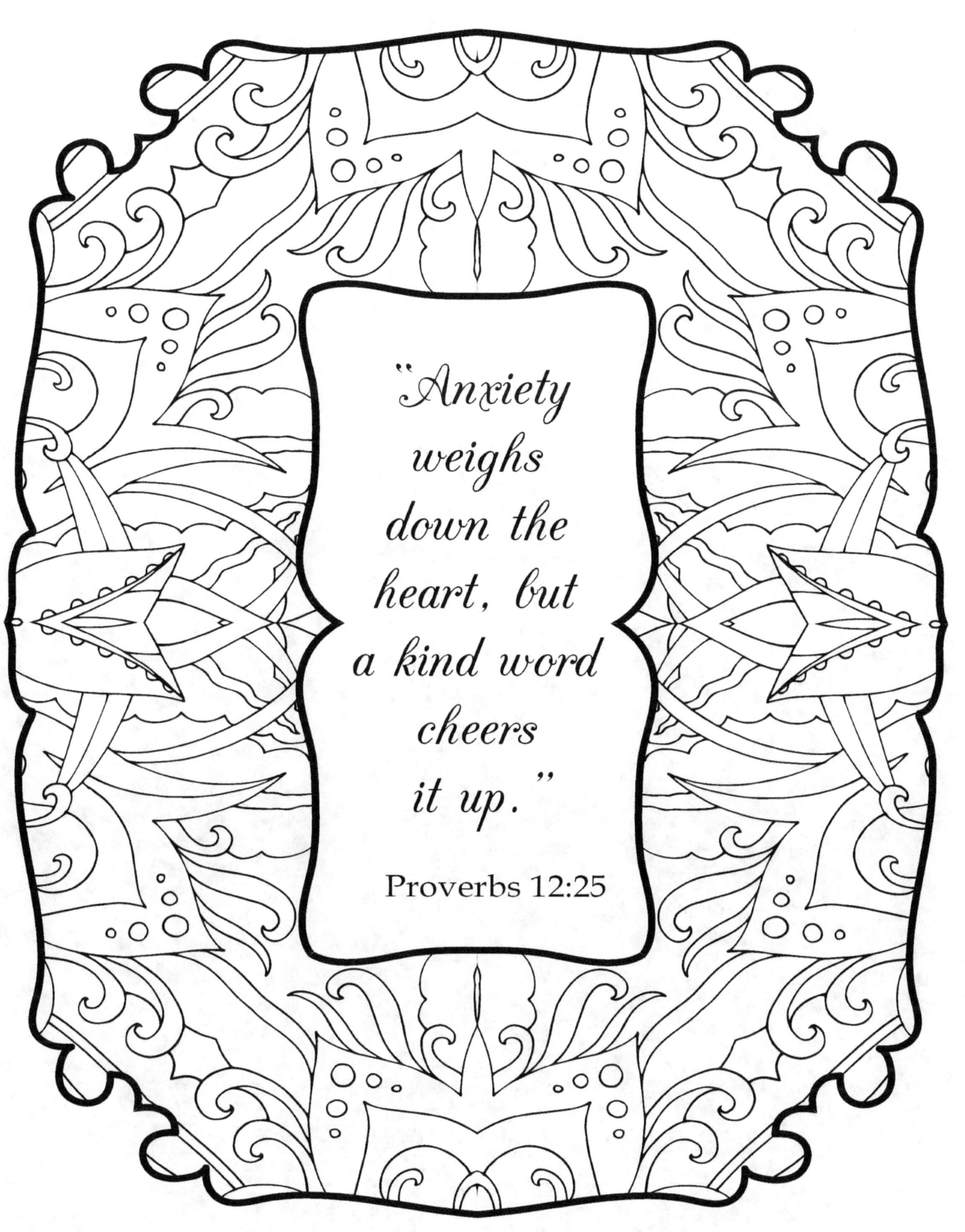

"Anxiety weighs down the heart, but a kind word cheers it up."

Proverbs 12:25

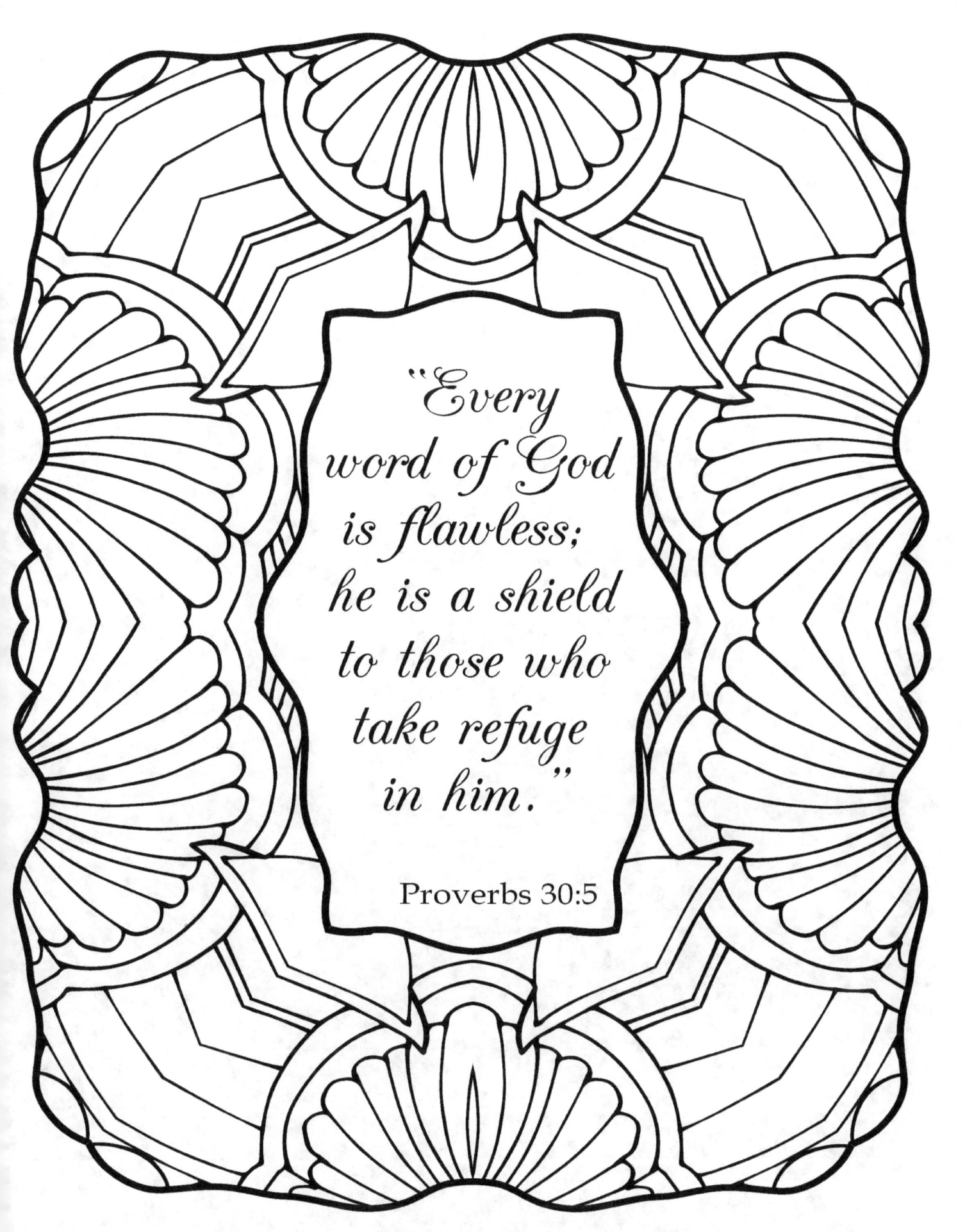

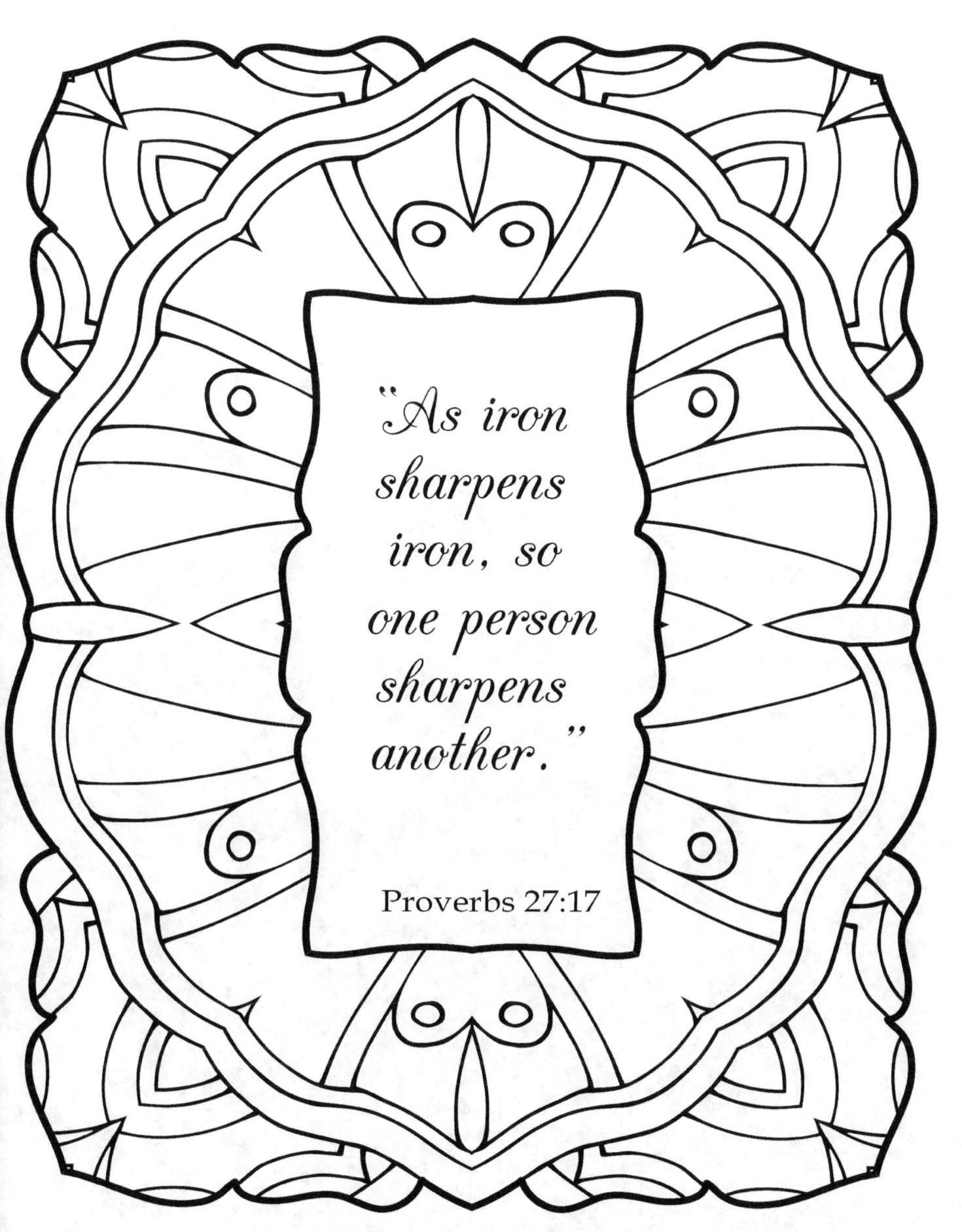

"As iron sharpens iron, so one person sharpens another."

Proverbs 27:17

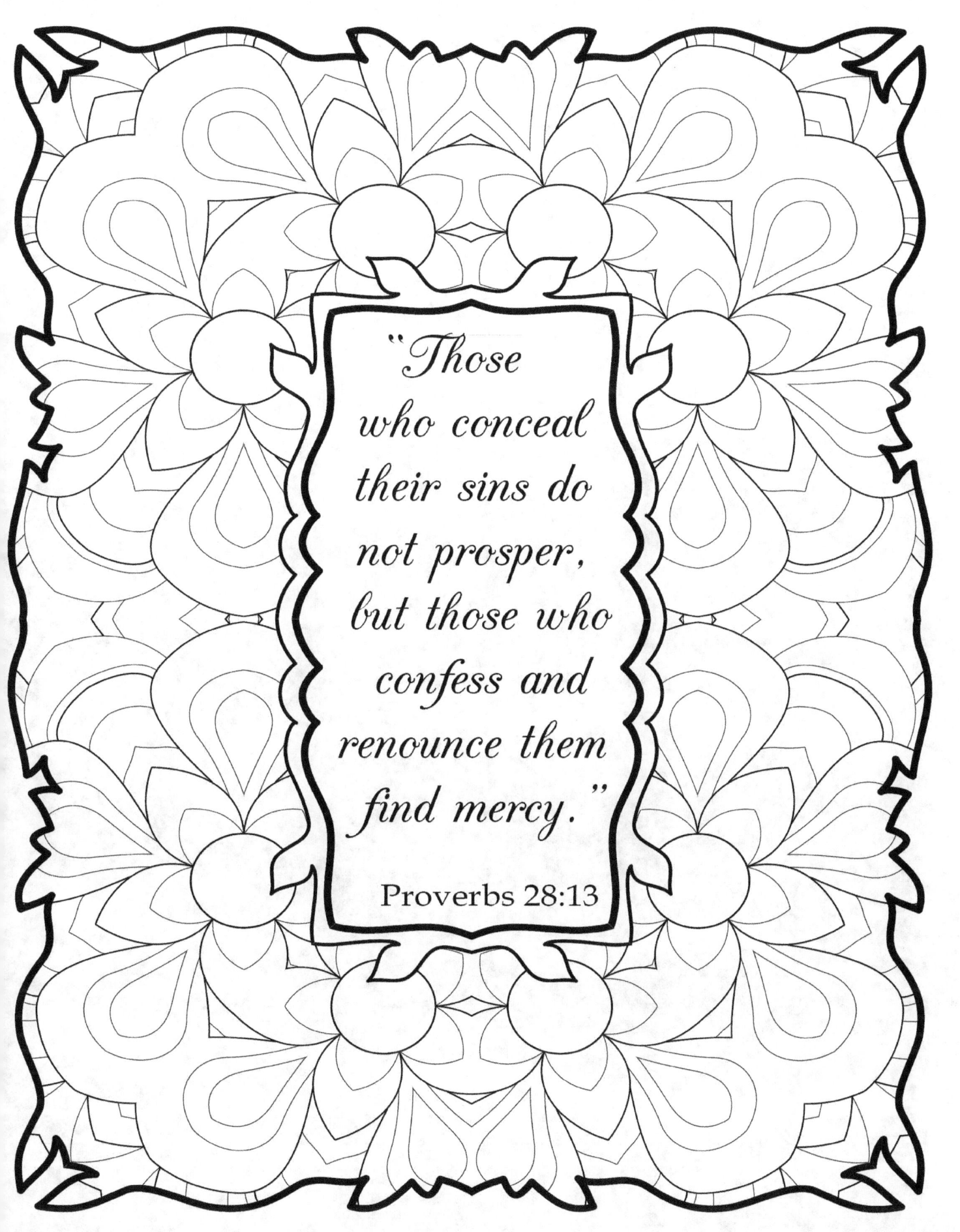

"Those who conceal their sins do not prosper, but those who confess and renounce them find mercy."

Proverbs 28:13

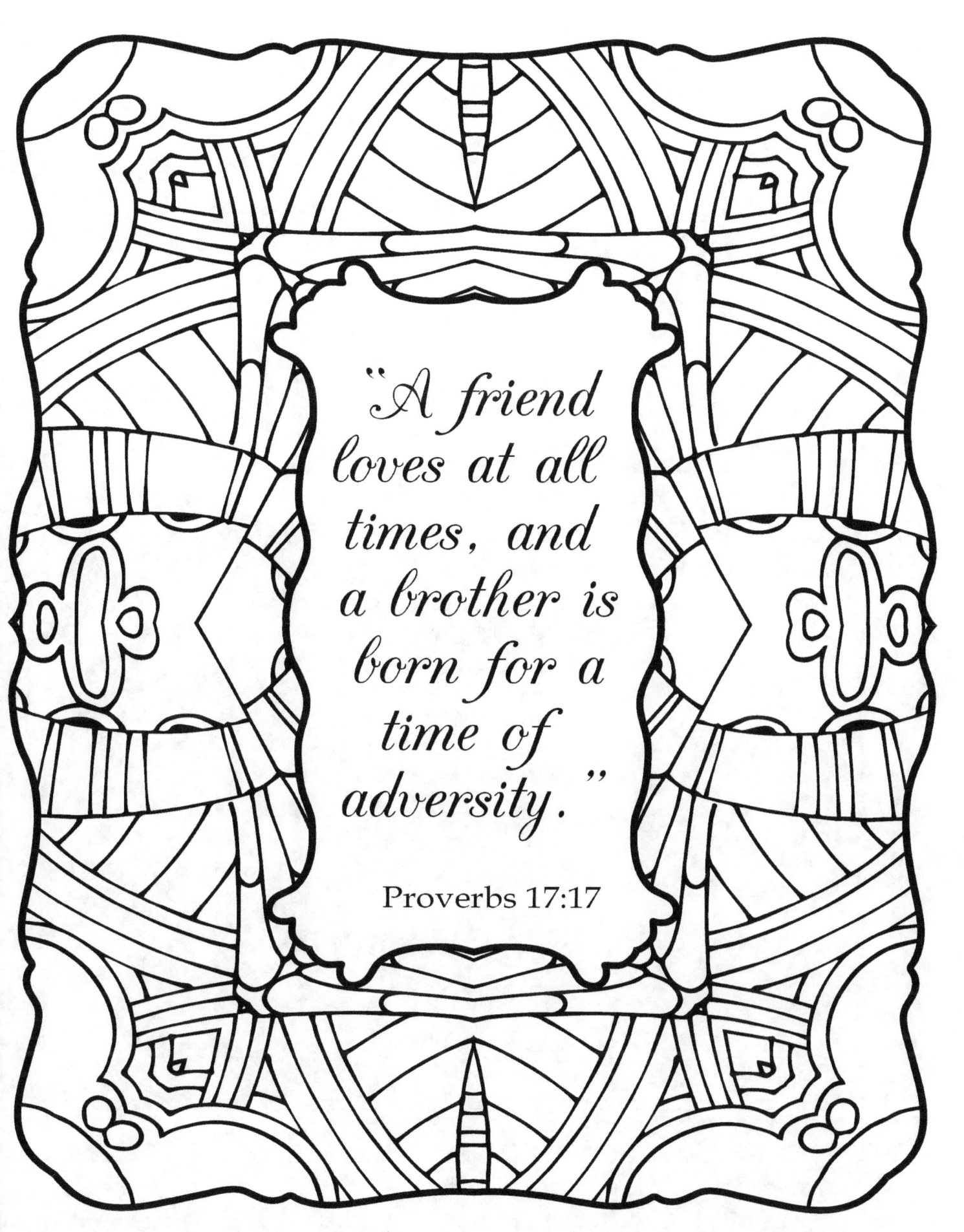

"A friend loves at all times, and a brother is born for a time of adversity."

Proverbs 17:17

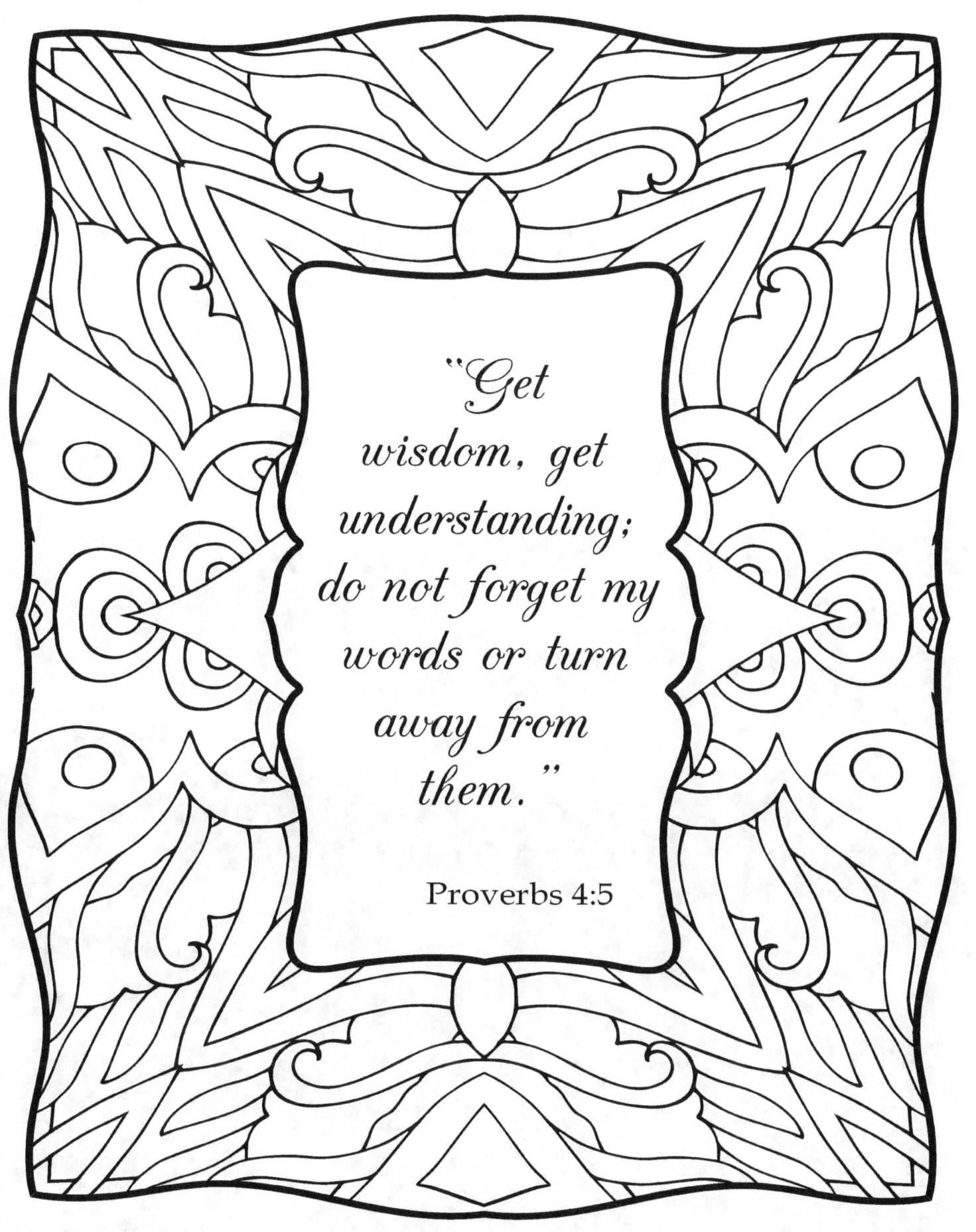

"Get wisdom, get understanding; do not forget my words or turn away from them."

Proverbs 4:5

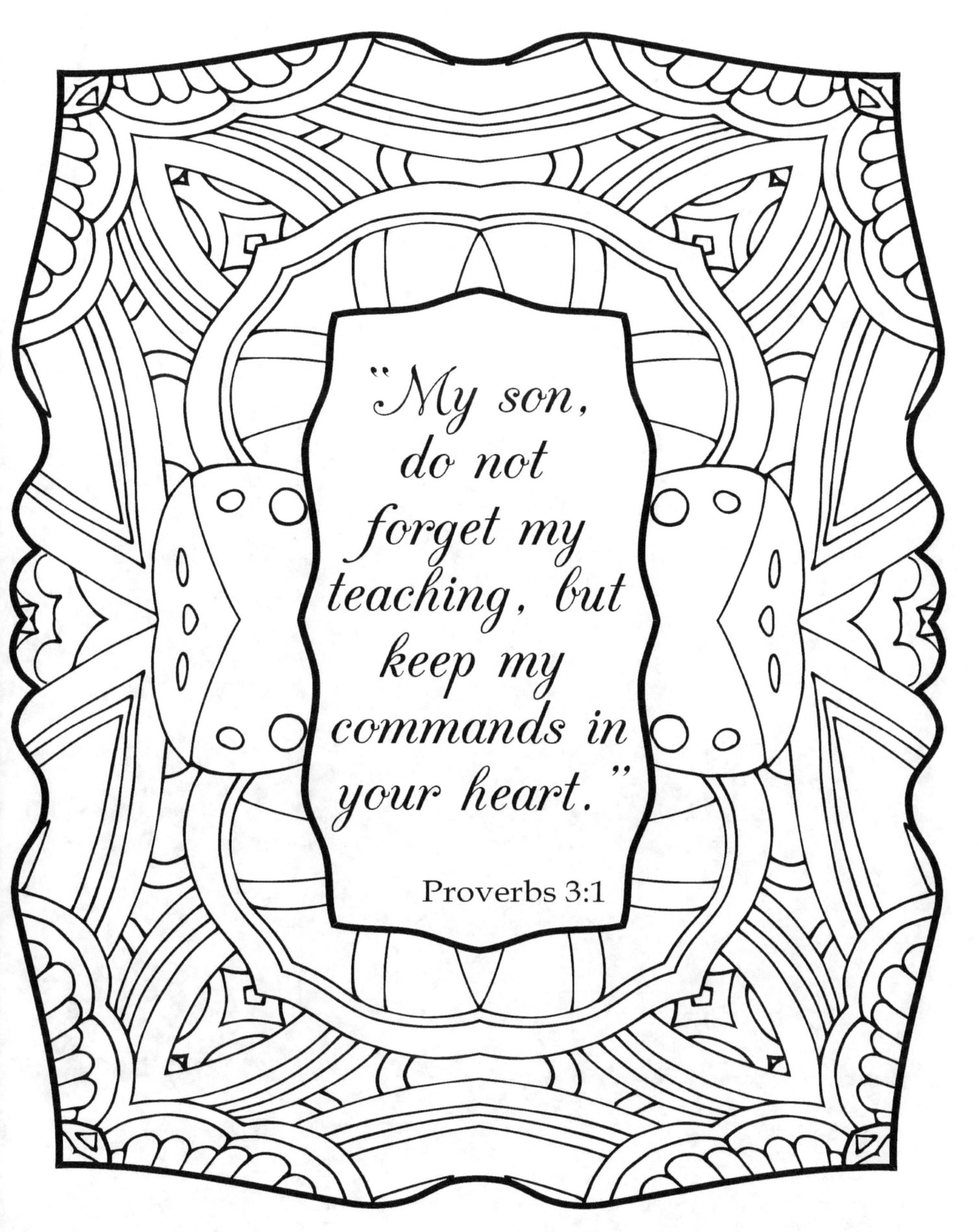

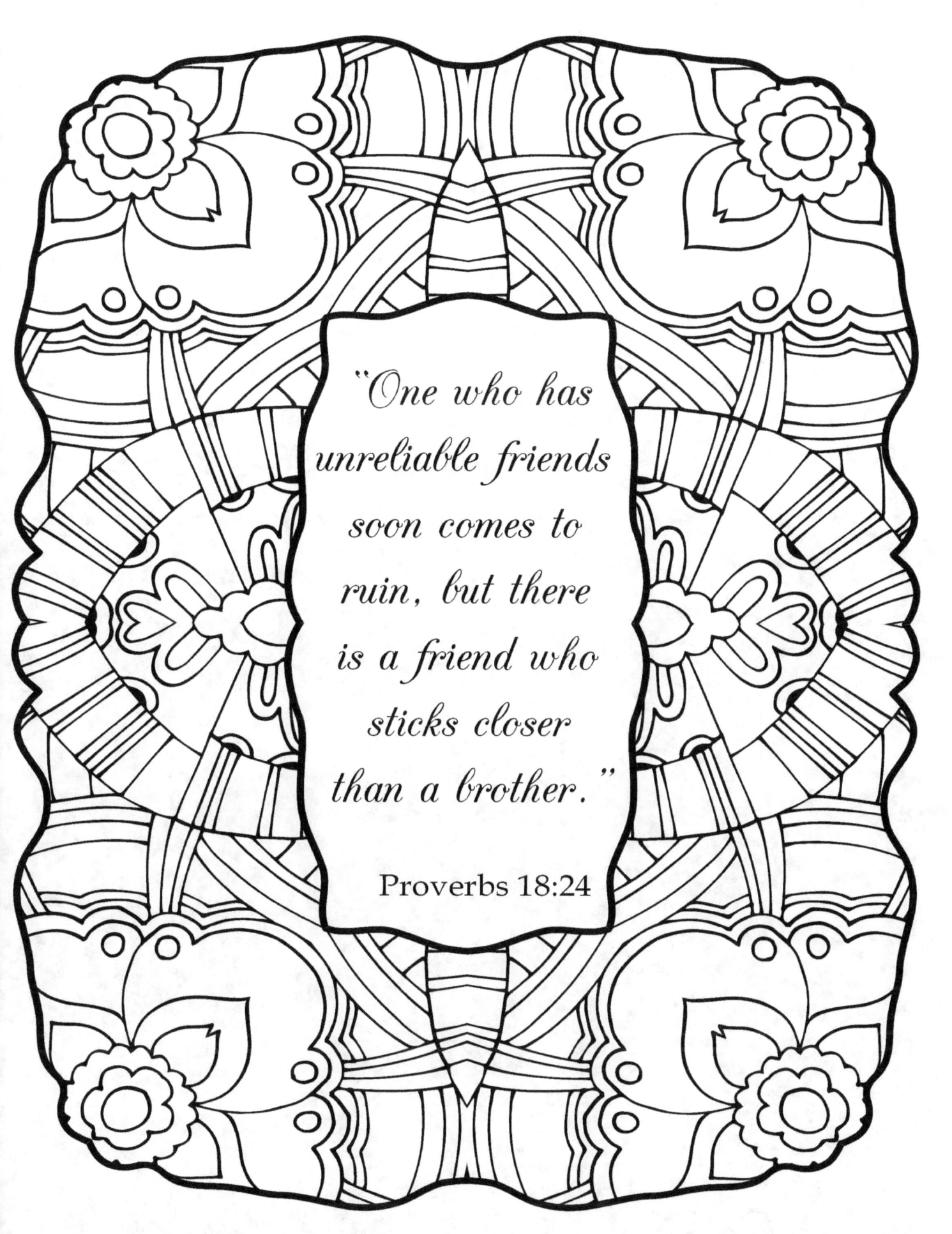

"One who has unreliable friends soon comes to ruin, but there is a friend who sticks closer than a brother."

Proverbs 18:24

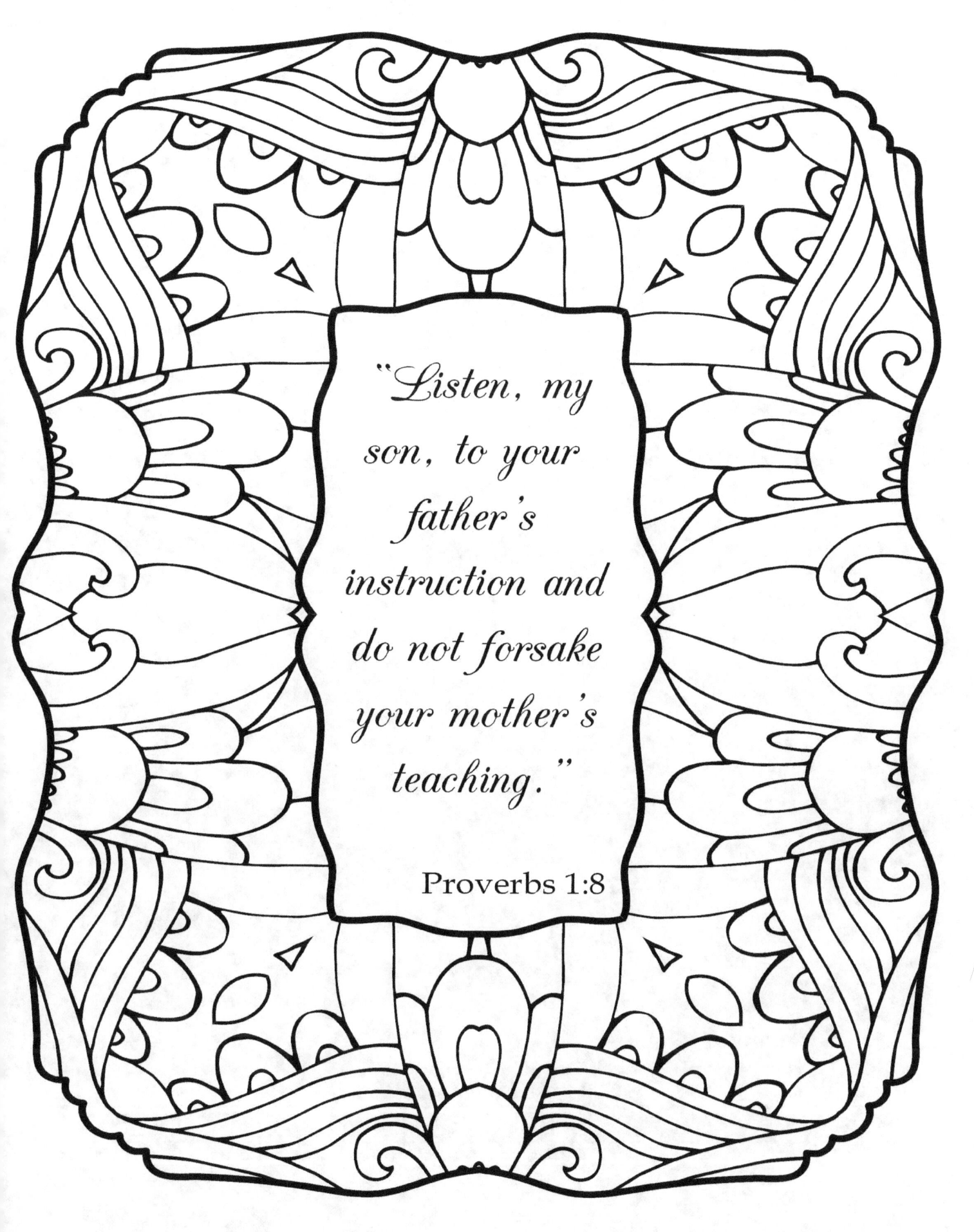

"Listen, my son, to your father's instruction and do not forsake your mother's teaching."

Proverbs 1:8

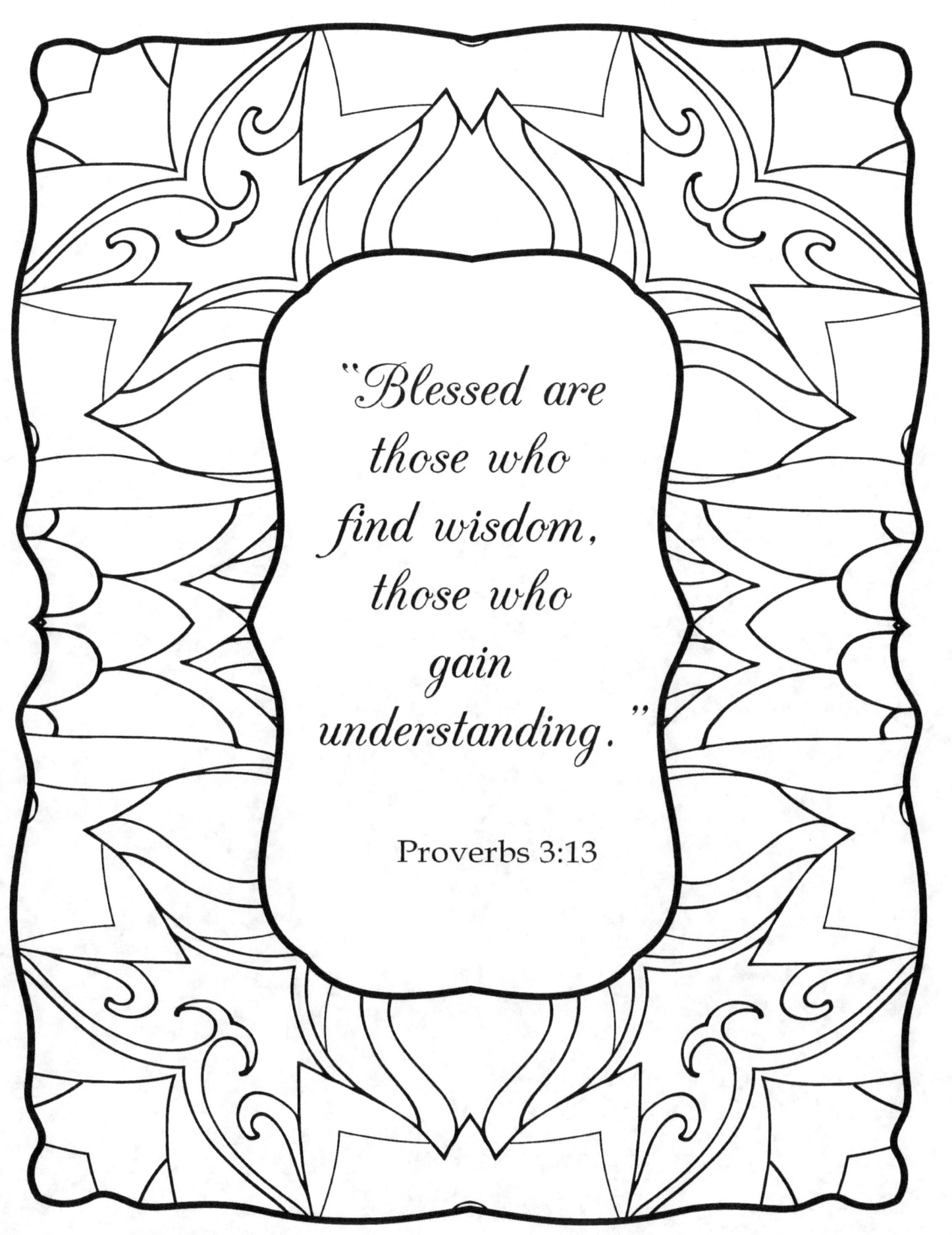

"Blessed are those who find wisdom, those who gain understanding."

Proverbs 3:13

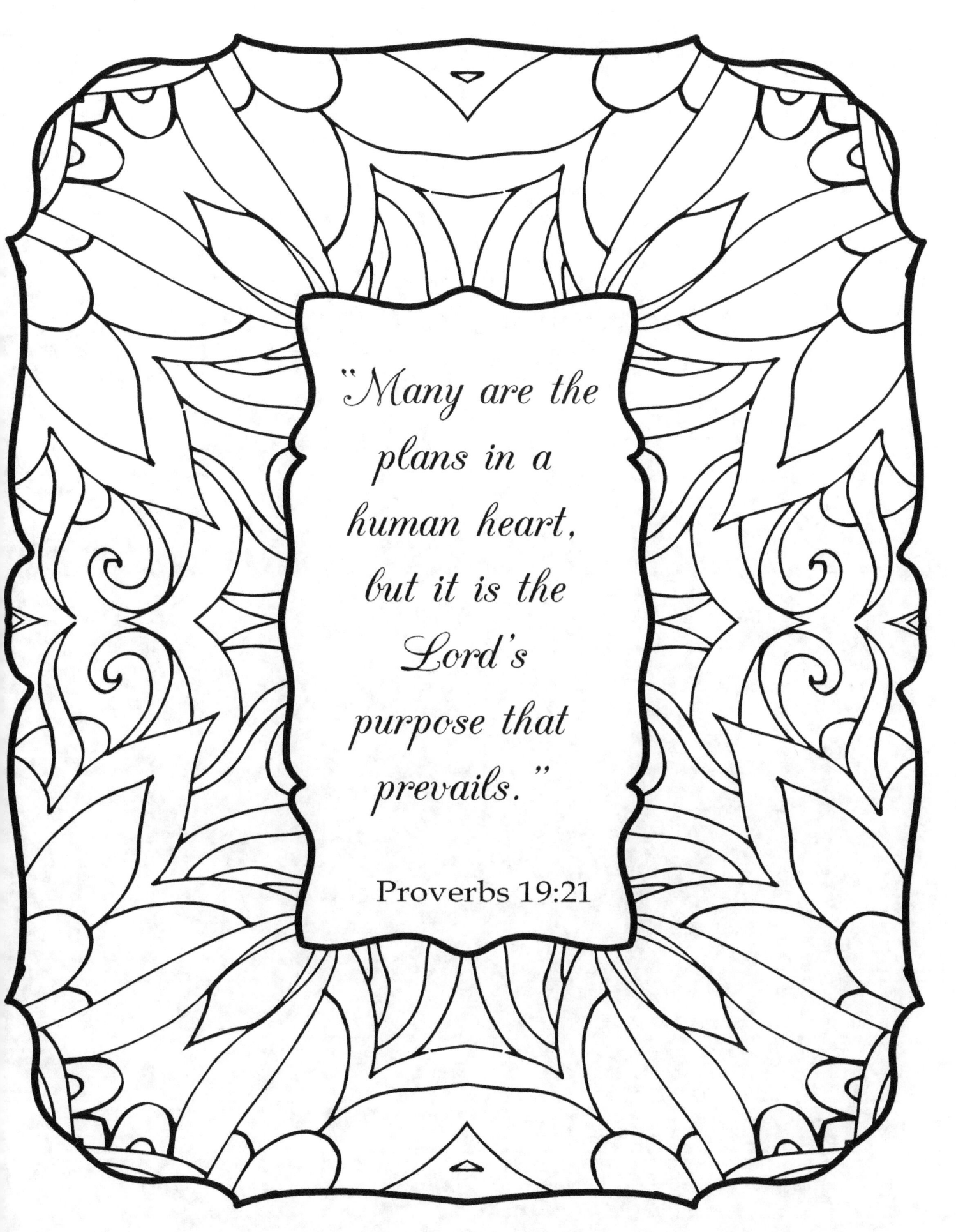

"Many are the plans in a human heart, but it is the Lord's purpose that prevails."

Proverbs 19:21

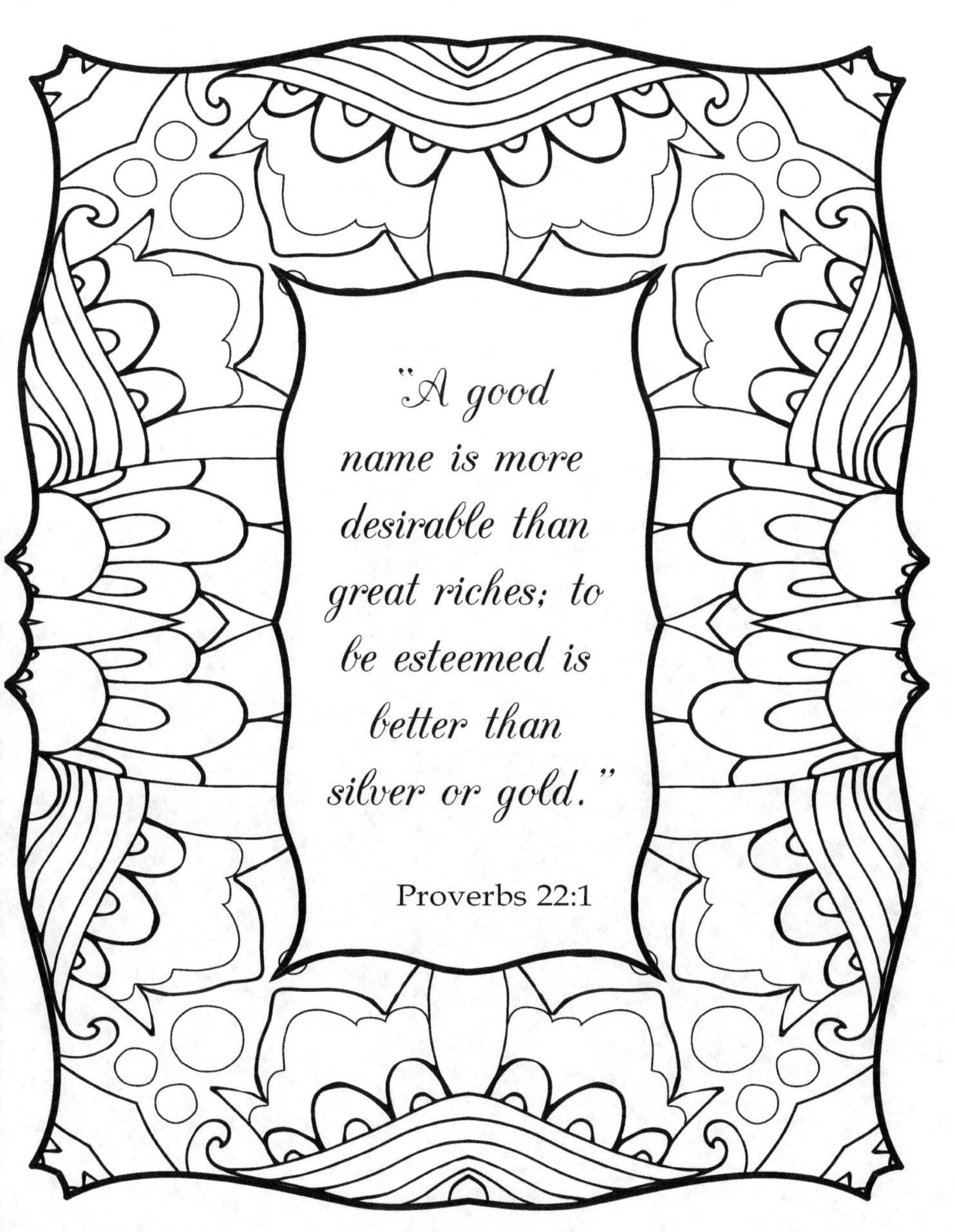

"A good name is more desirable than great riches; to be esteemed is better than silver or gold."

Proverbs 22:1

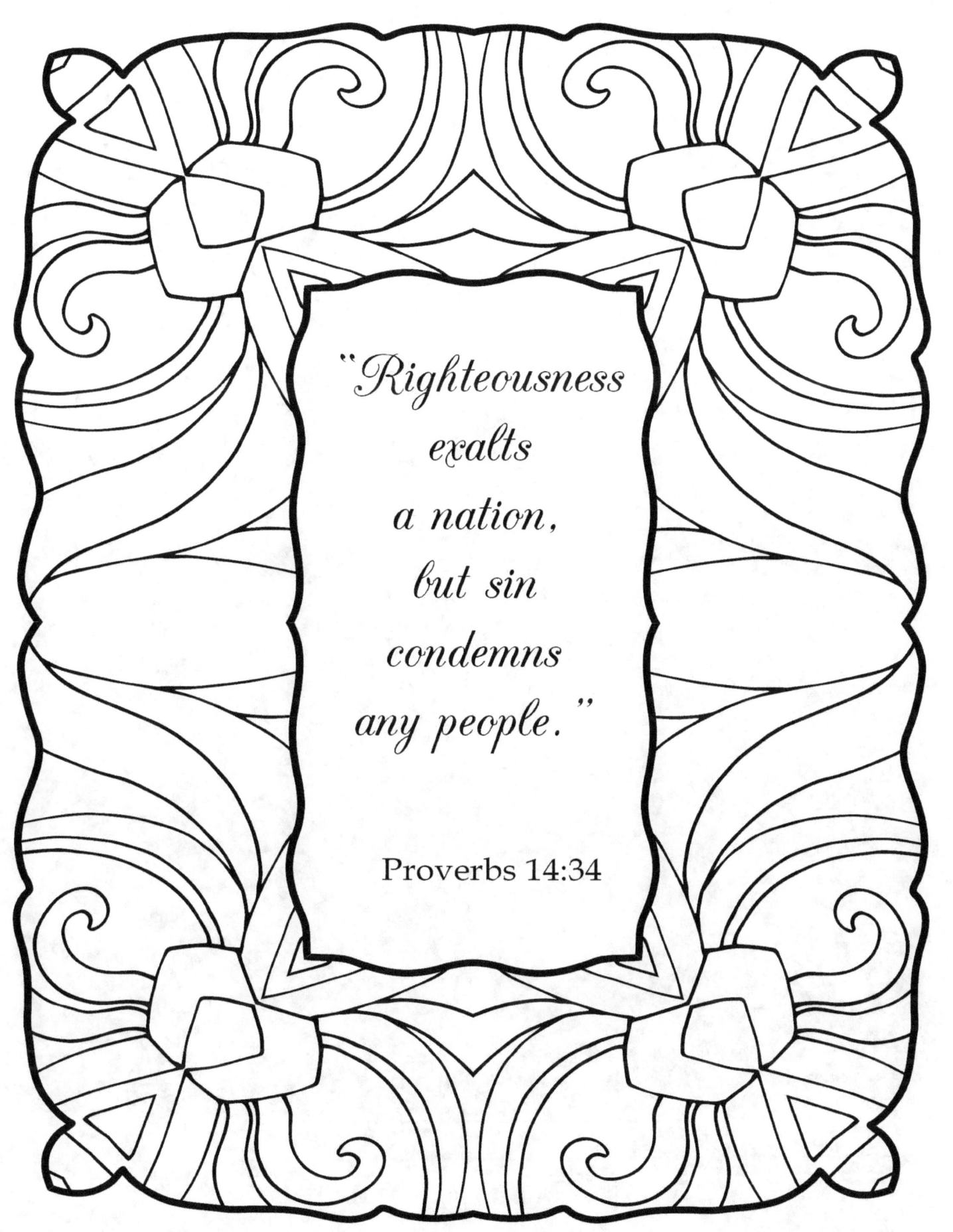

"Righteousness exalts a nation, but sin condemns any people."

Proverbs 14:34

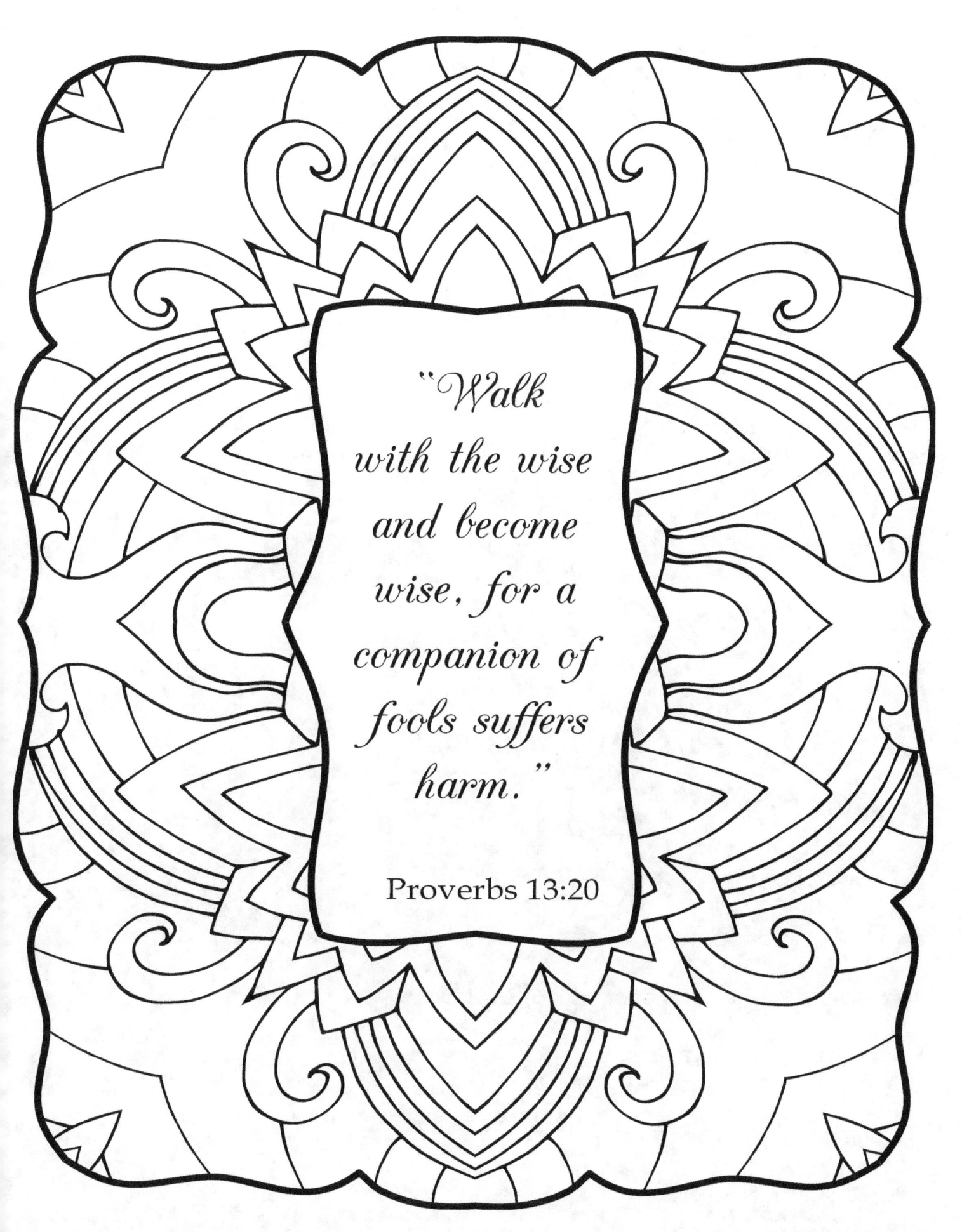

"Walk with the wise and become wise, for a companion of fools suffers harm."

Proverbs 13:20

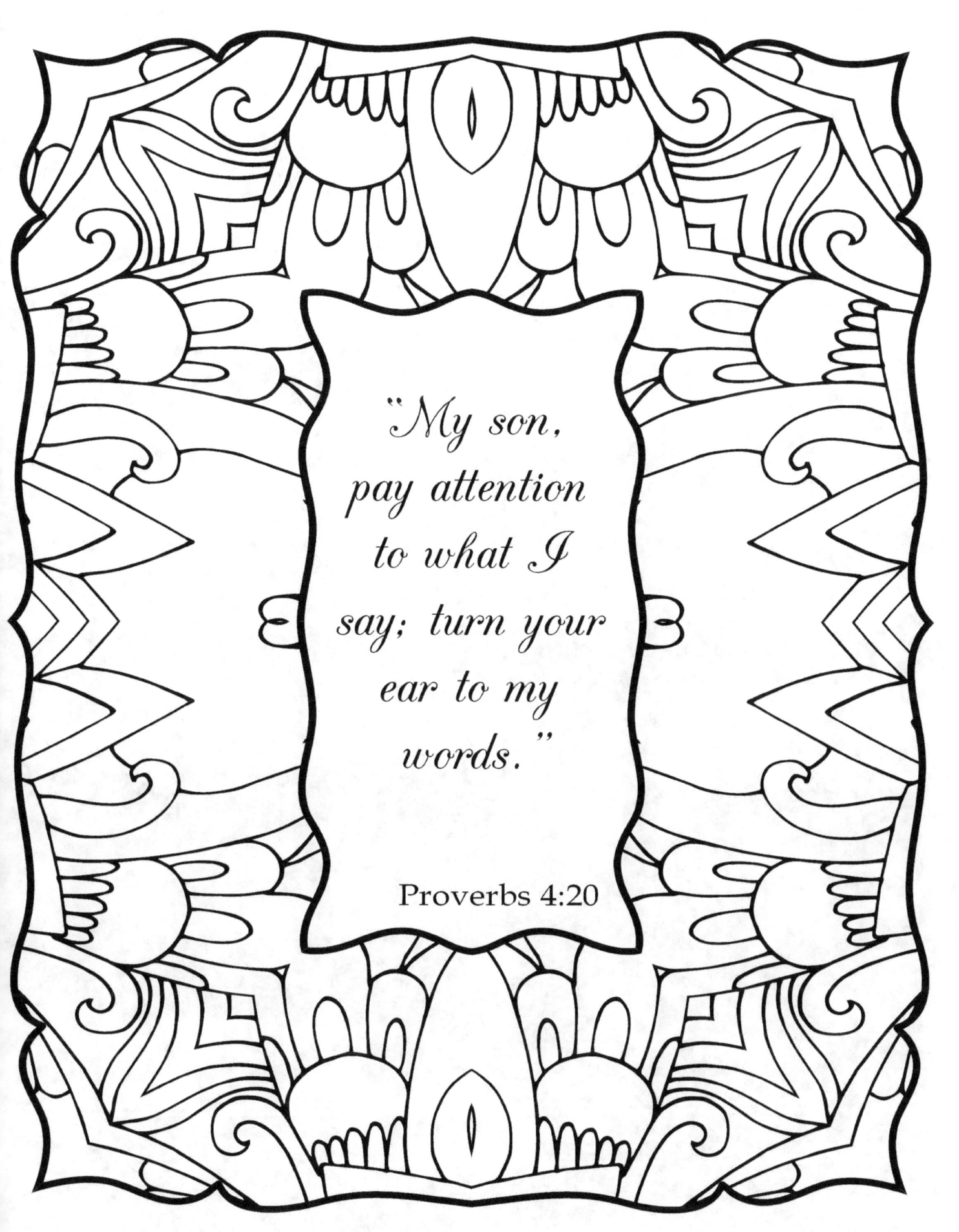

"My son, pay attention to what I say; turn your ear to my words."

Proverbs 4:20

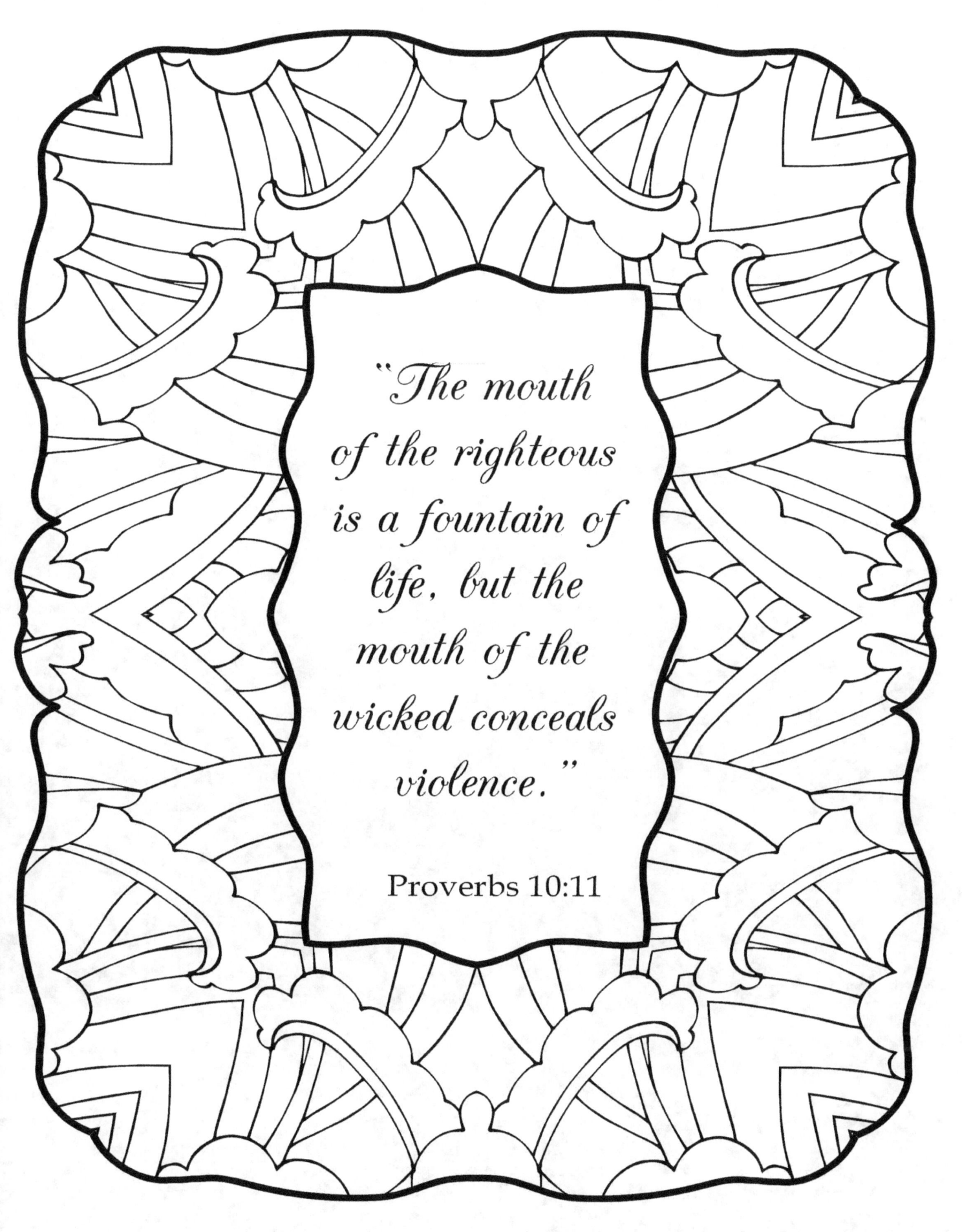

"The mouth of the righteous is a fountain of life, but the mouth of the wicked conceals violence."

Proverbs 10:11

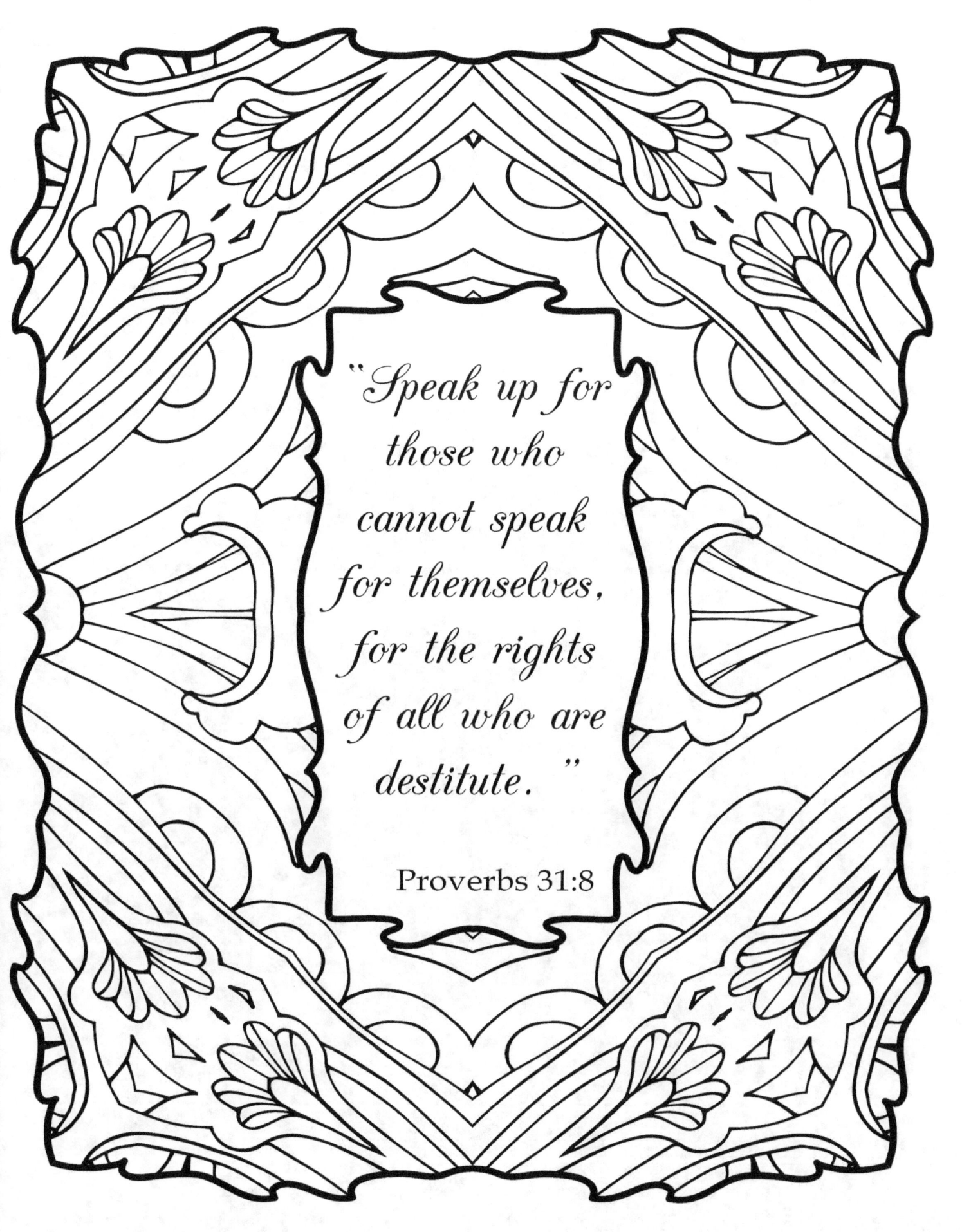

"Speak up for those who cannot speak for themselves, for the rights of all who are destitute."

Proverbs 31:8

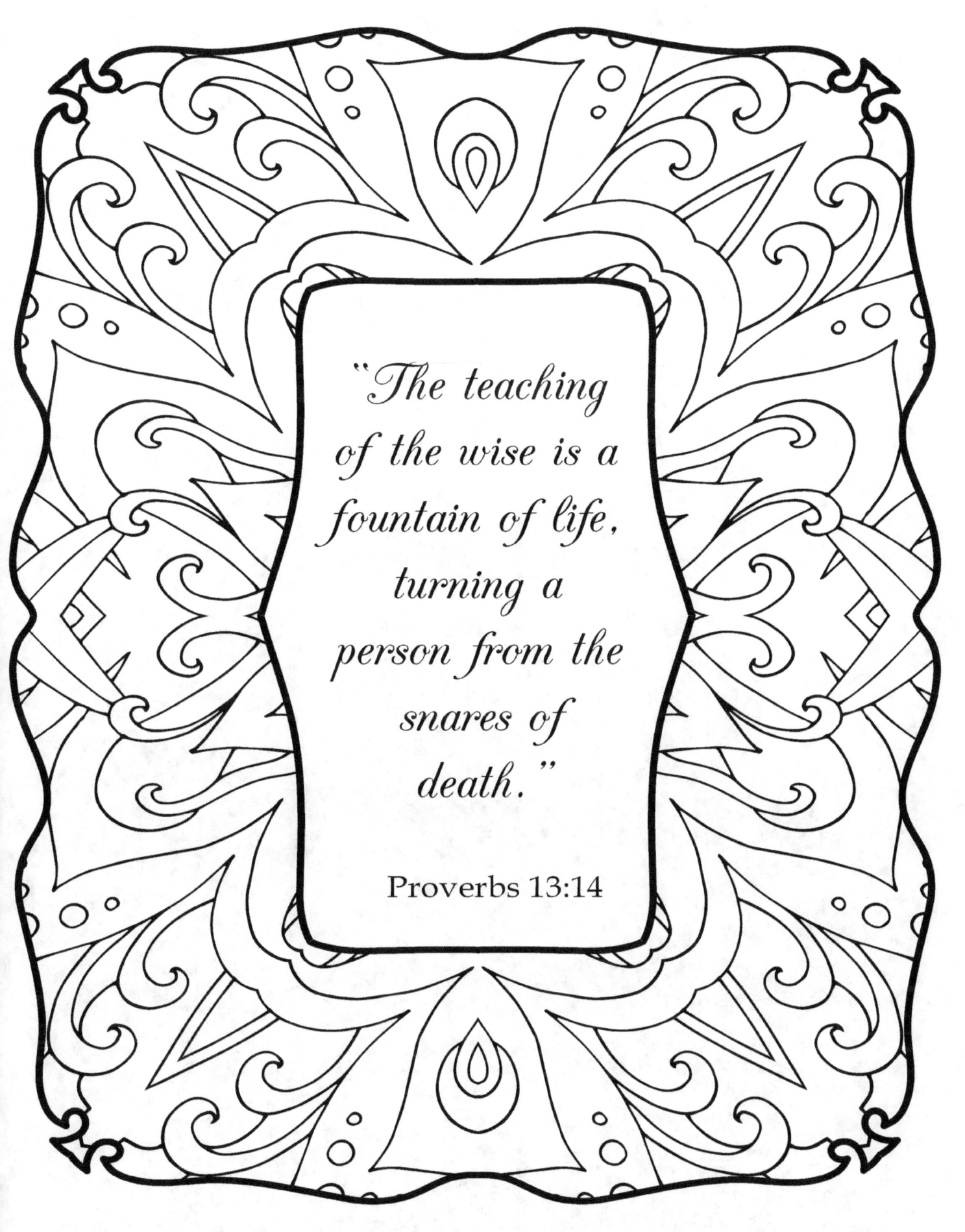

"The teaching of the wise is a fountain of life, turning a person from the snares of death."

Proverbs 13:14

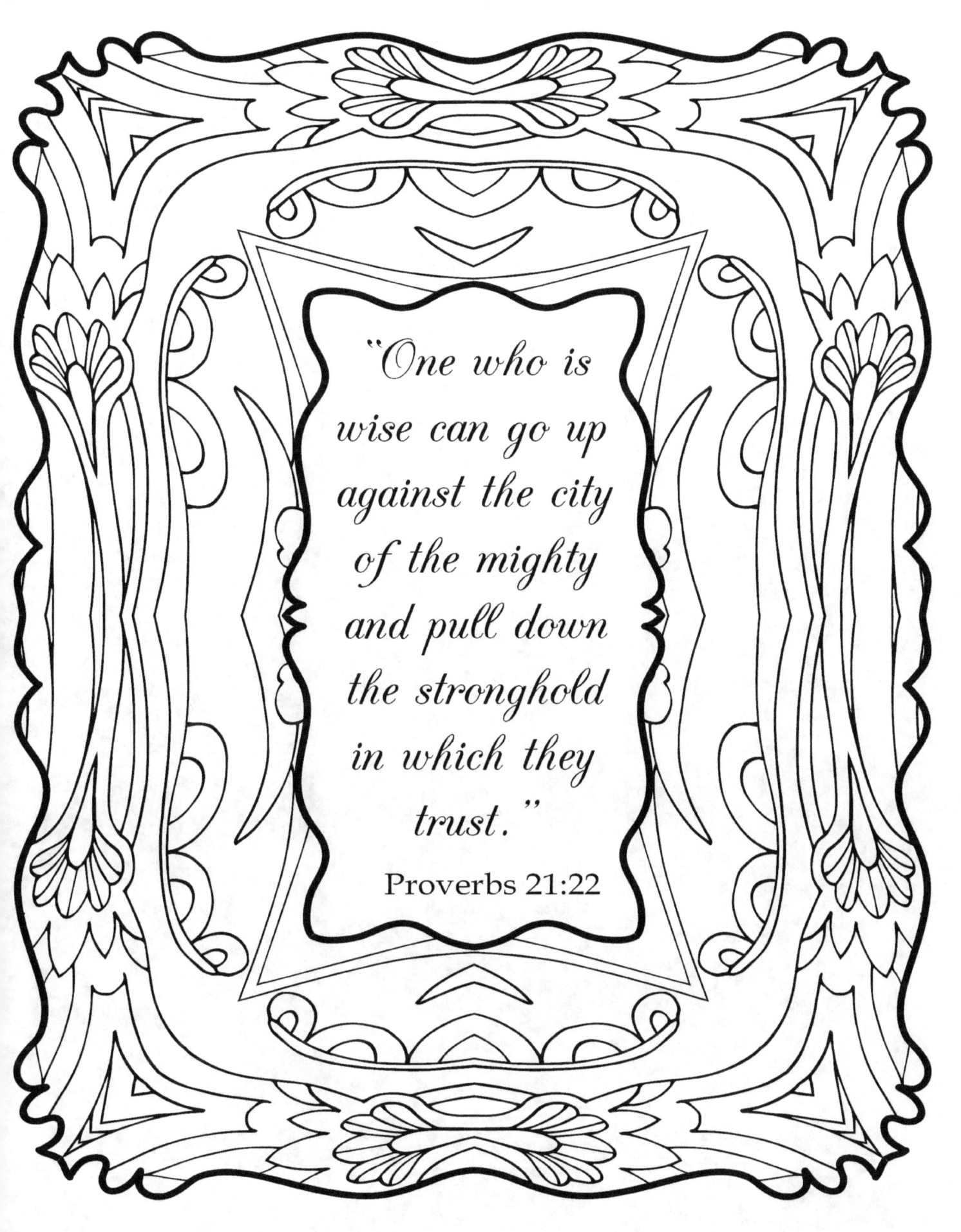

"One who is wise can go up against the city of the mighty and pull down the stronghold in which they trust."

Proverbs 21:22

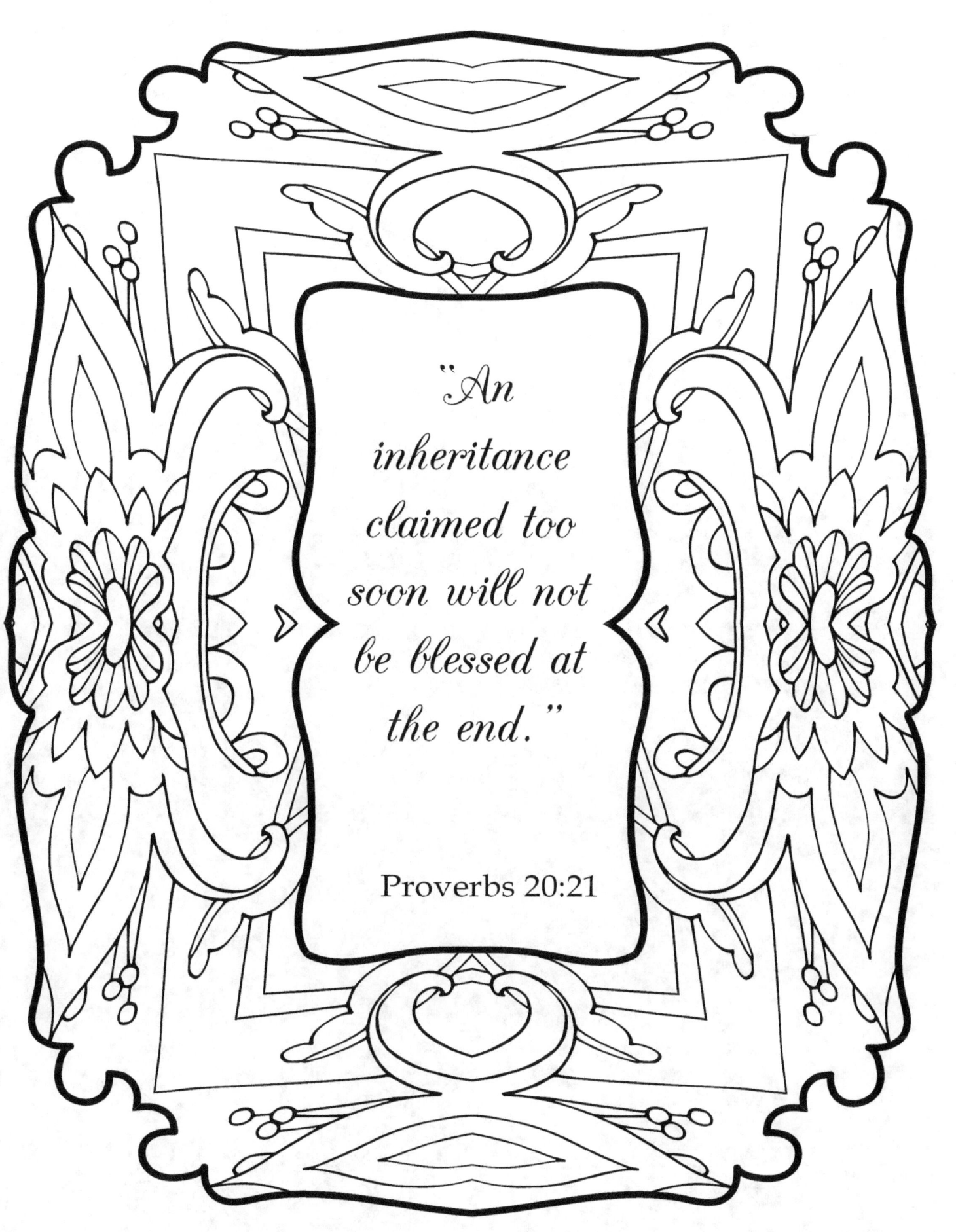

"An inheritance claimed too soon will not be blessed at the end."

Proverbs 20:21

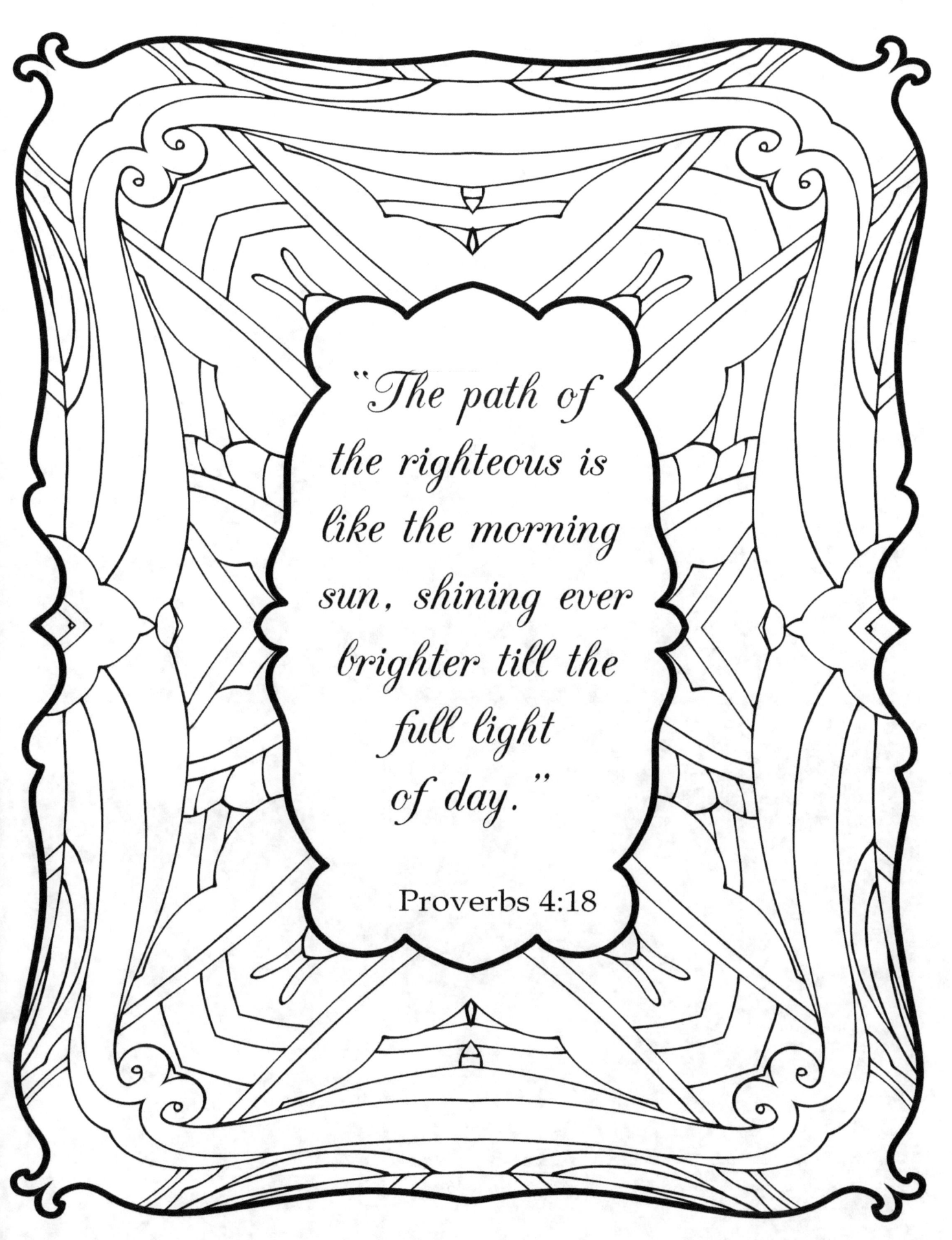

"The path of the righteous is like the morning sun, shining ever brighter till the full light of day."

Proverbs 4:18

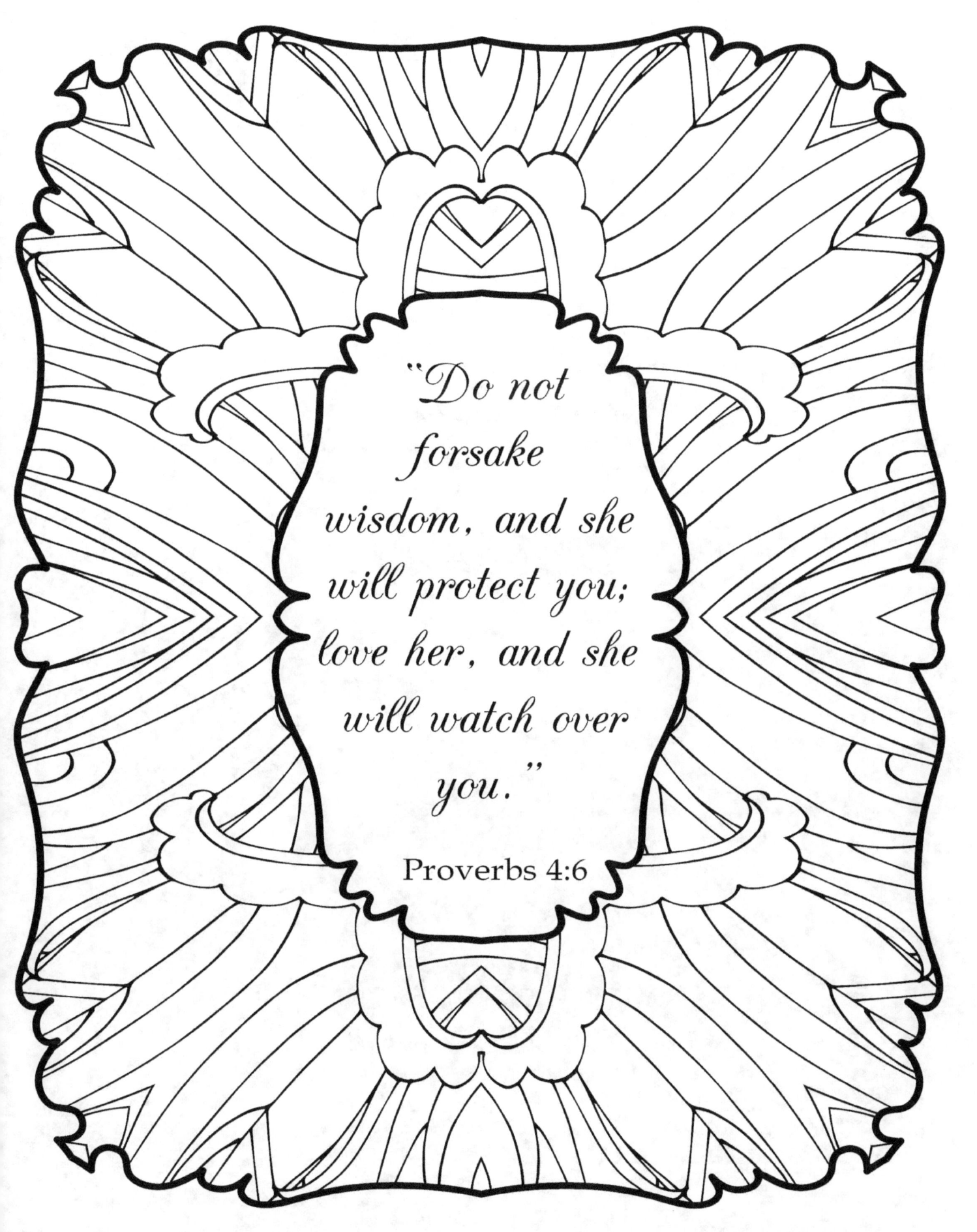

"Do not forsake wisdom, and she will protect you; love her, and she will watch over you."

Proverbs 4:6

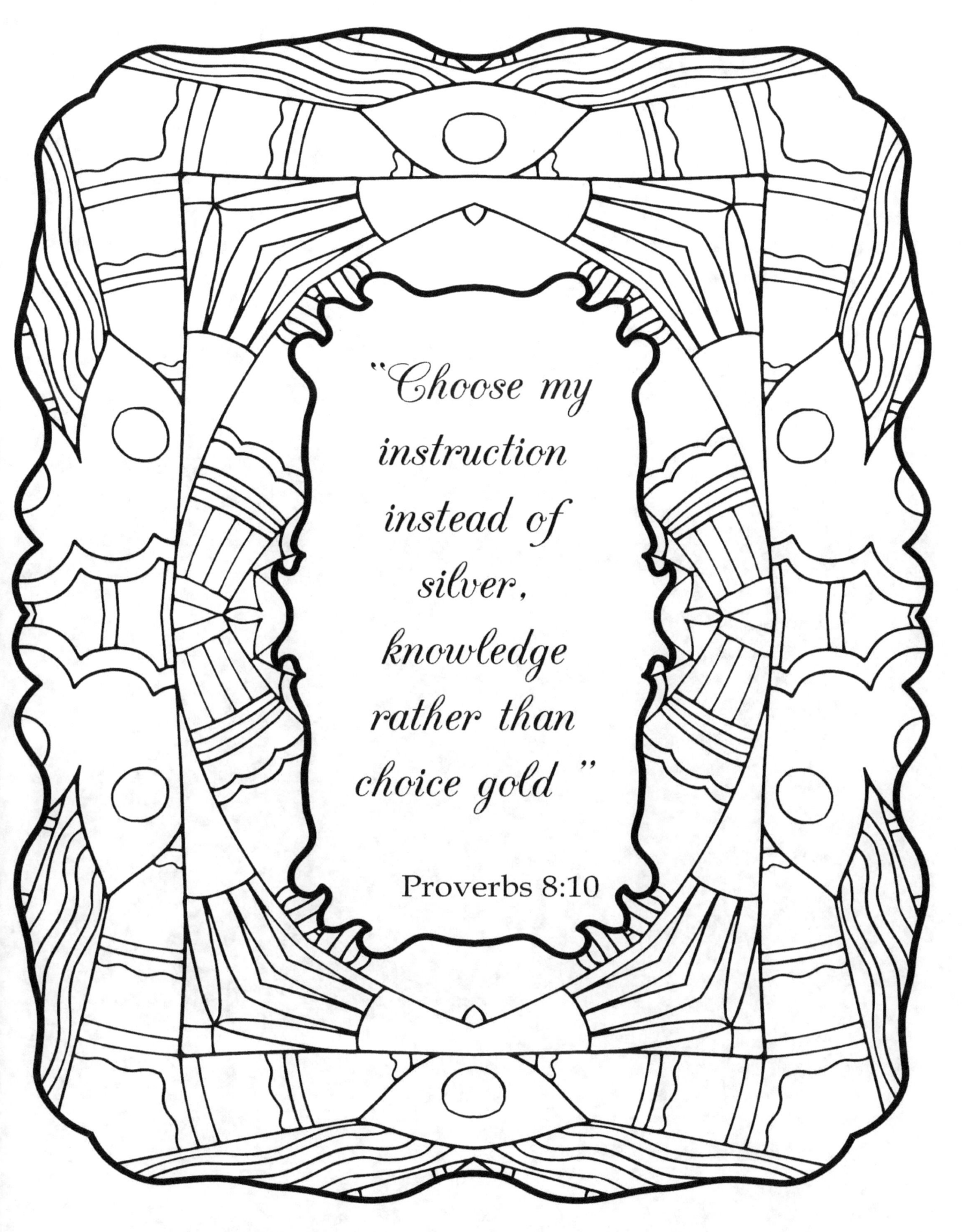

"Choose my instruction instead of silver, knowledge rather than choice gold"

Proverbs 8:10

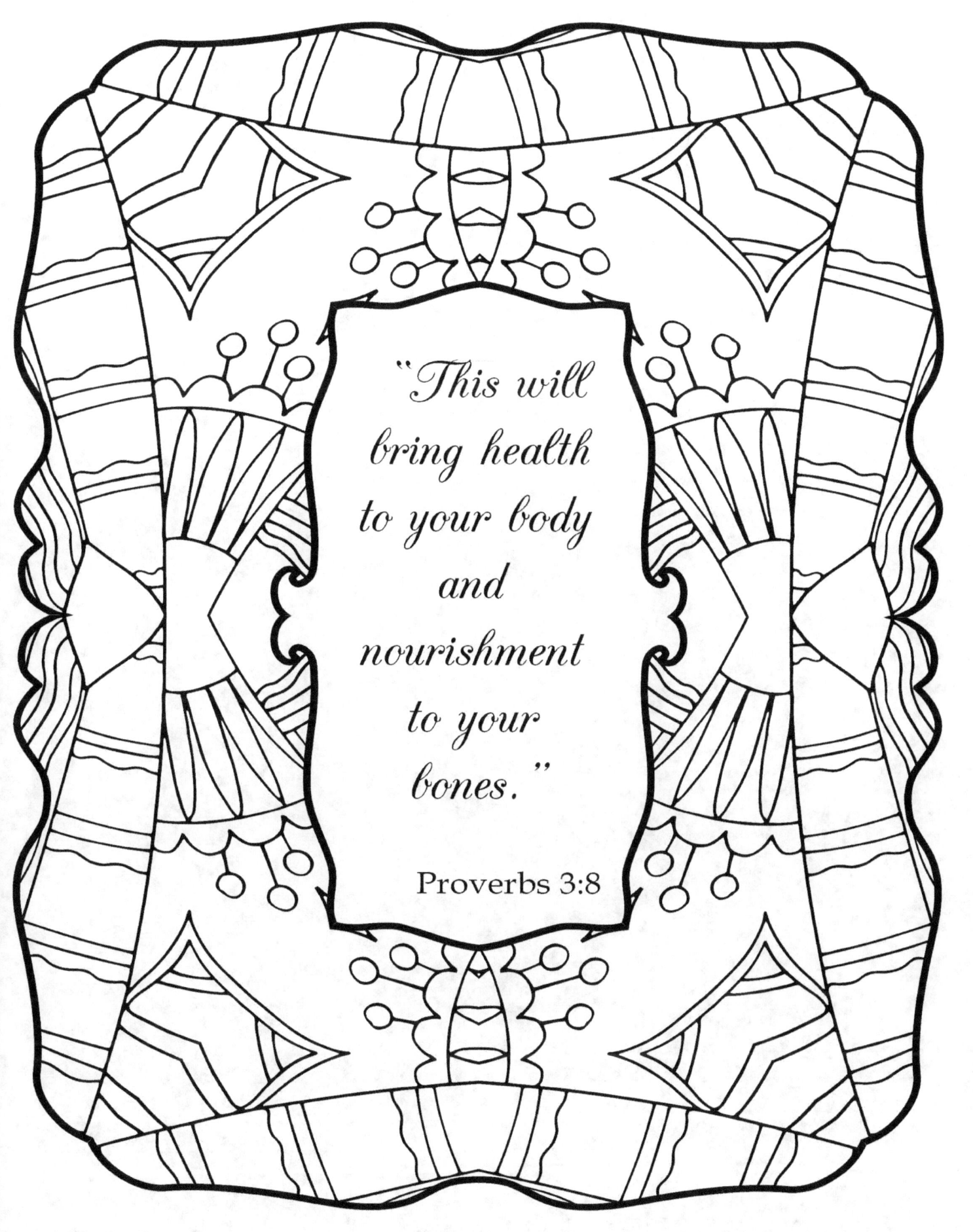

"This will bring health to your body and nourishment to your bones."

Proverbs 3:8

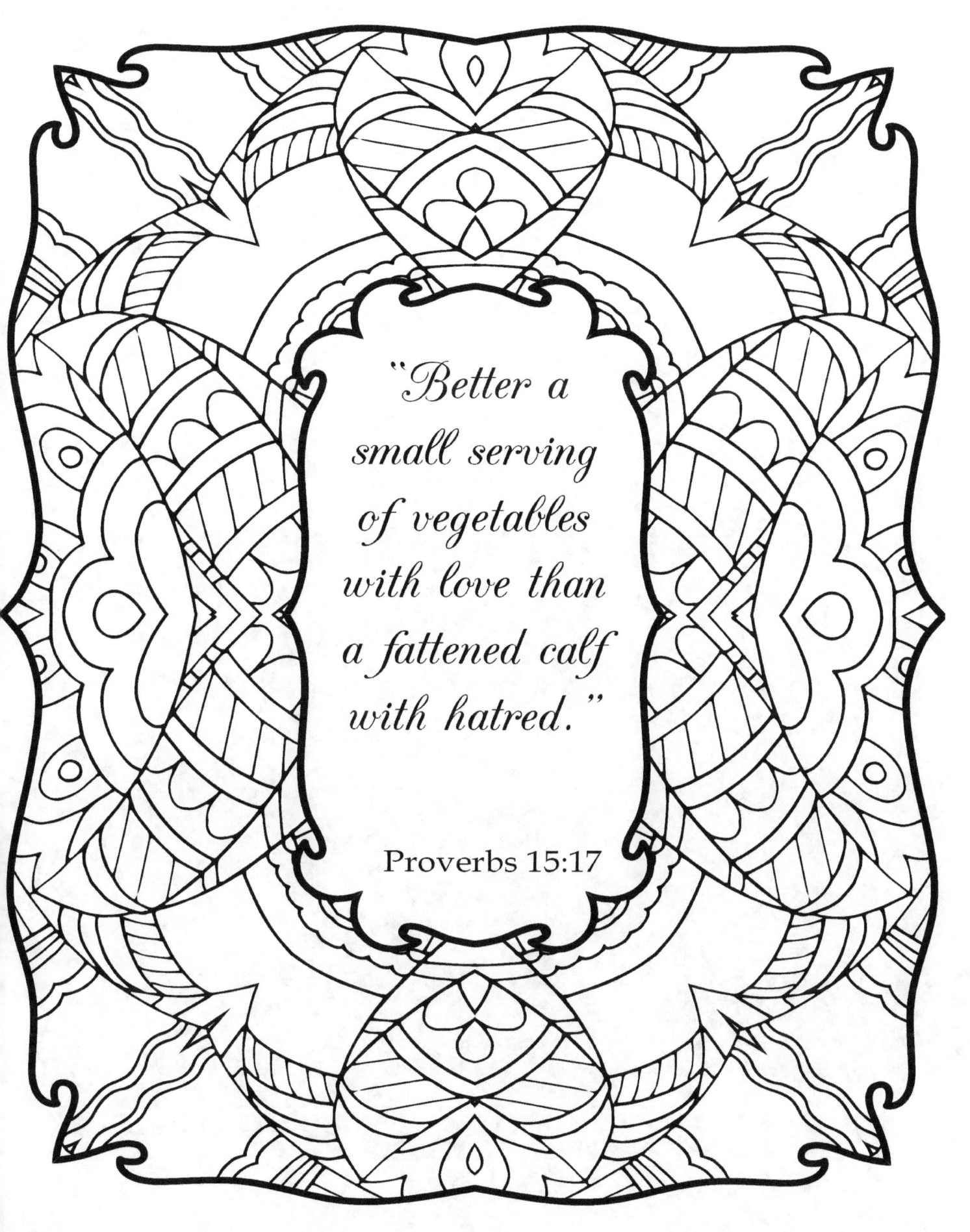

"Better a small serving of vegetables with love than a fattened calf with hatred."

Proverbs 15:17

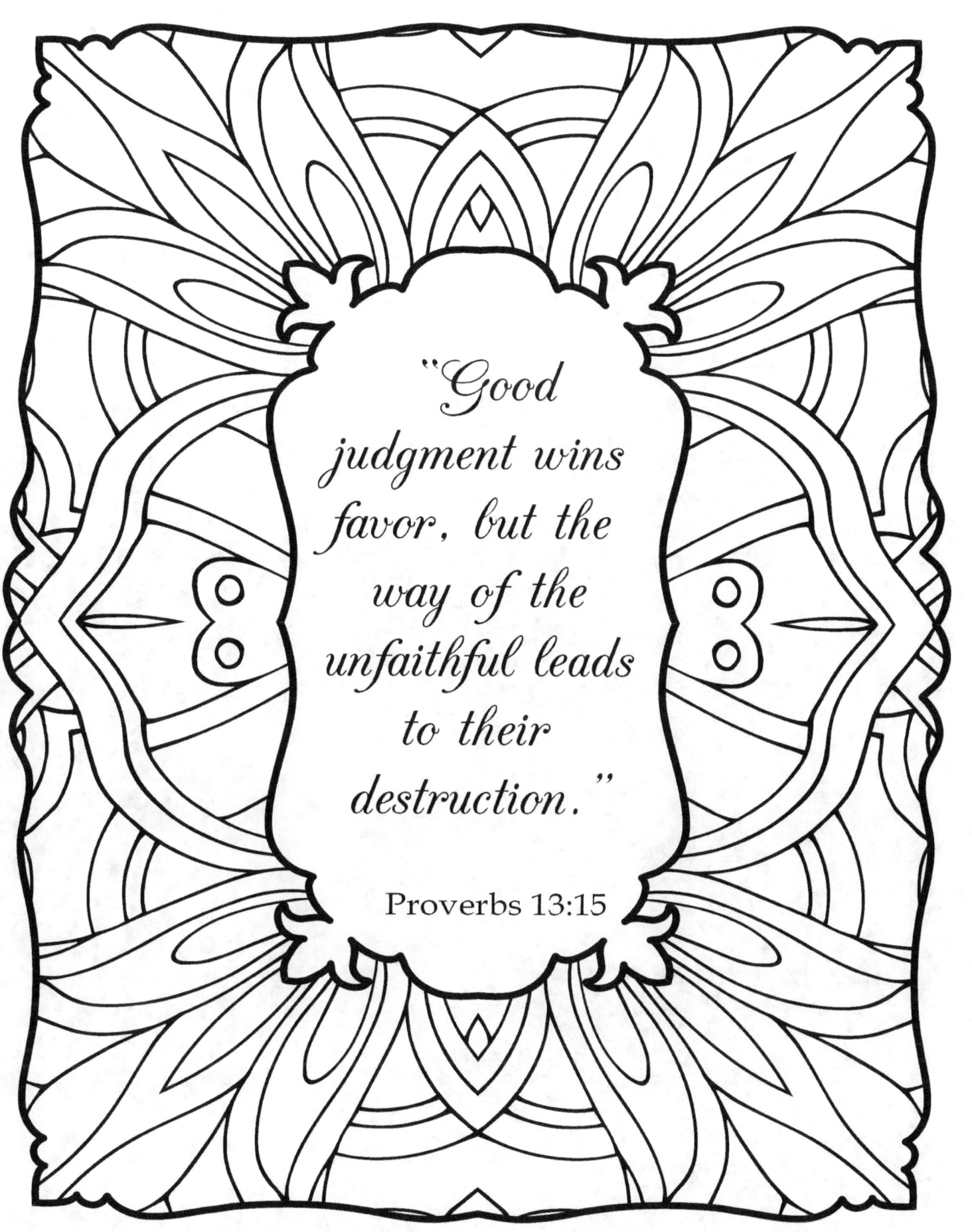

"Good judgment wins favor, but the way of the unfaithful leads to their destruction."

Proverbs 13:15

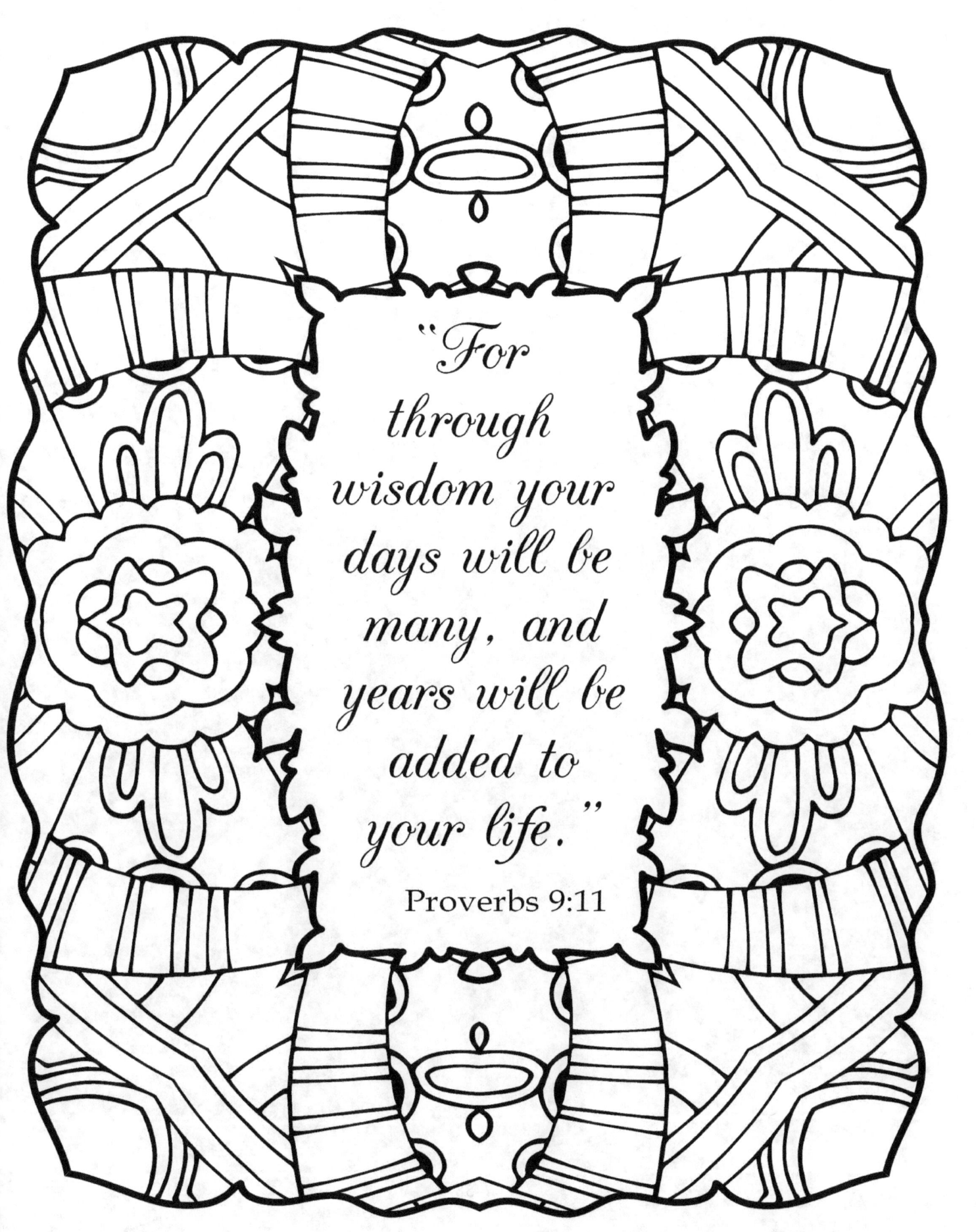

"For through wisdom your days will be many, and years will be added to your life."

Proverbs 9:11

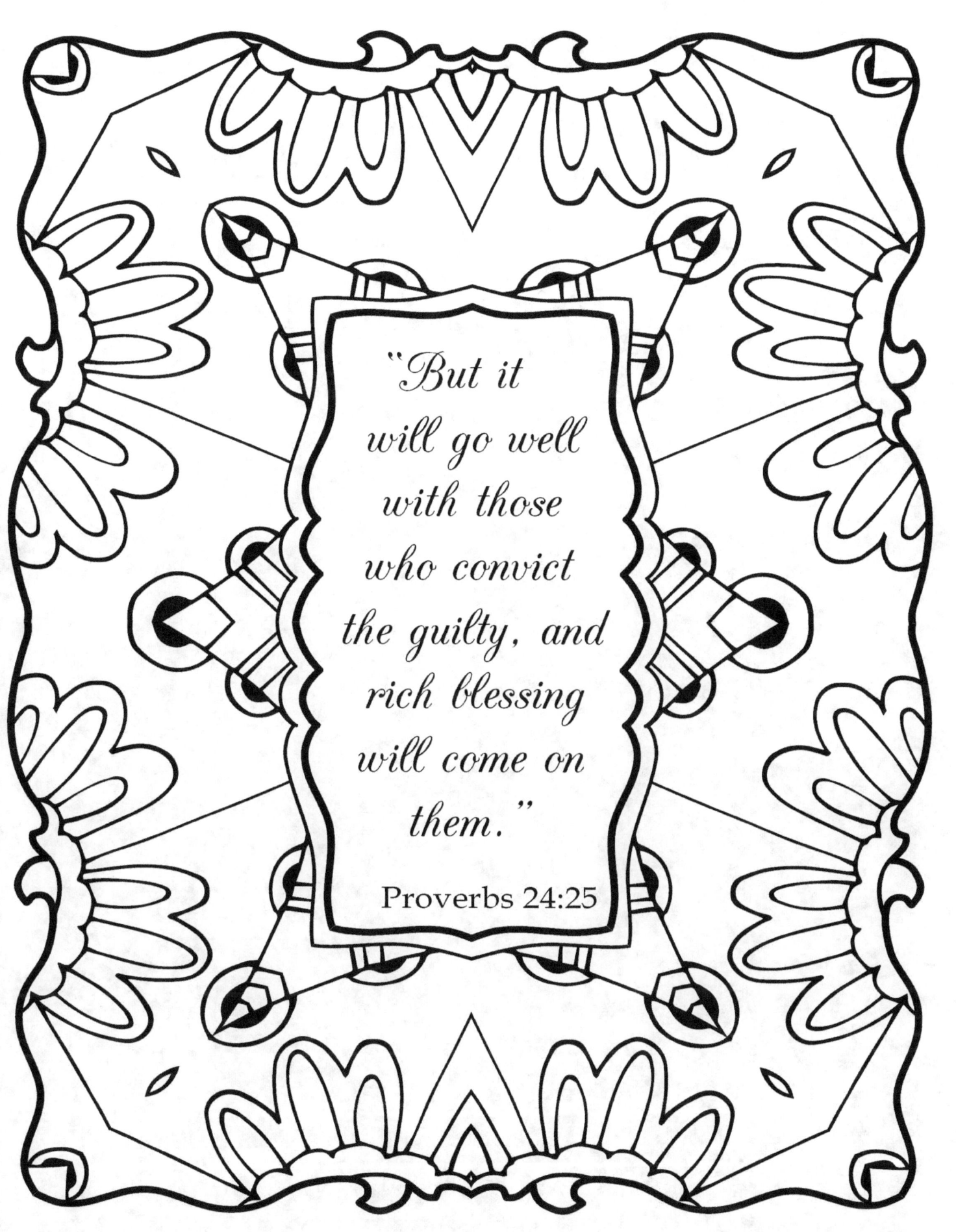

"But it will go well with those who convict the guilty, and rich blessing will come on them."

Proverbs 24:25

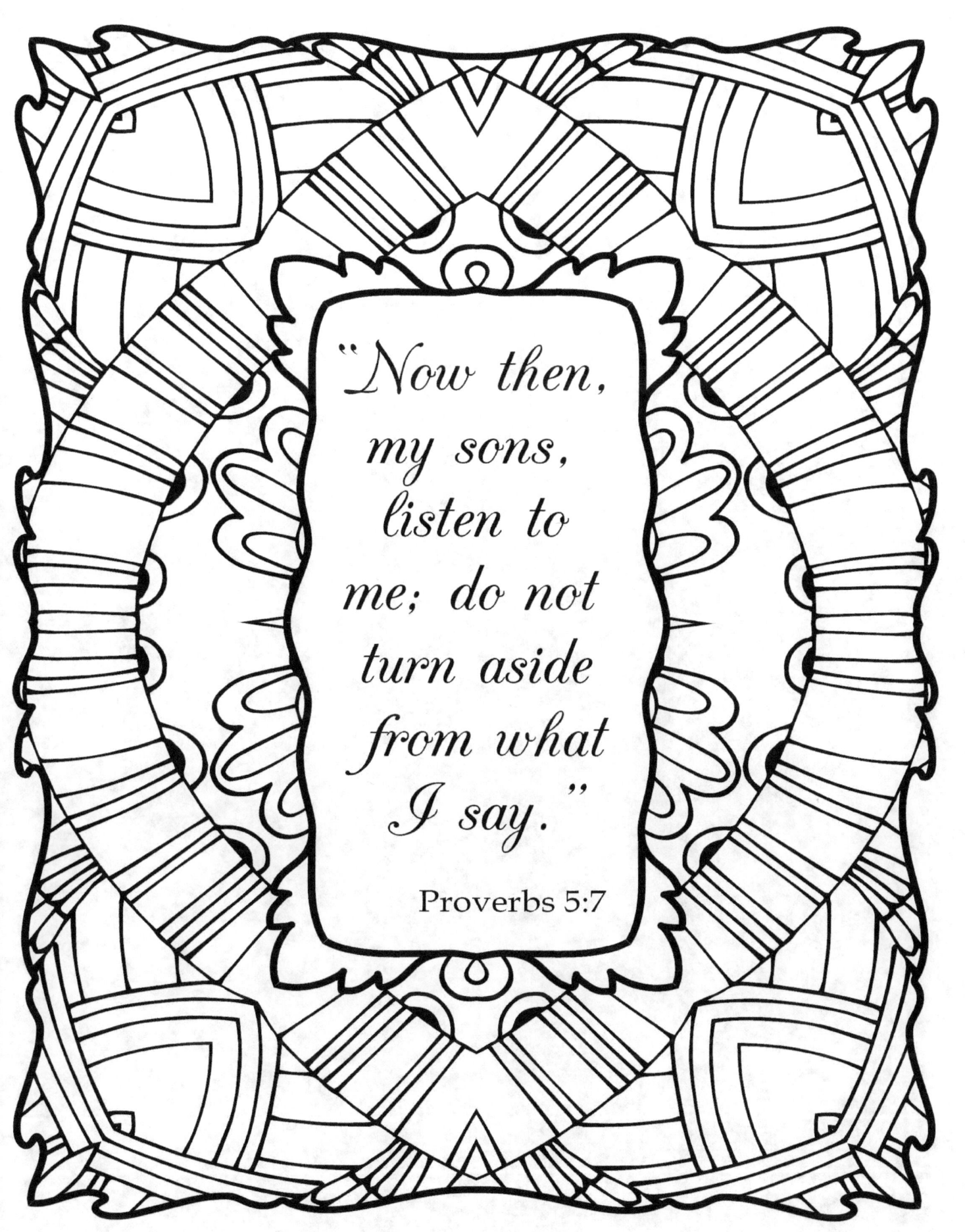

"Now then, my sons, listen to me; do not turn aside from what I say."

Proverbs 5:7

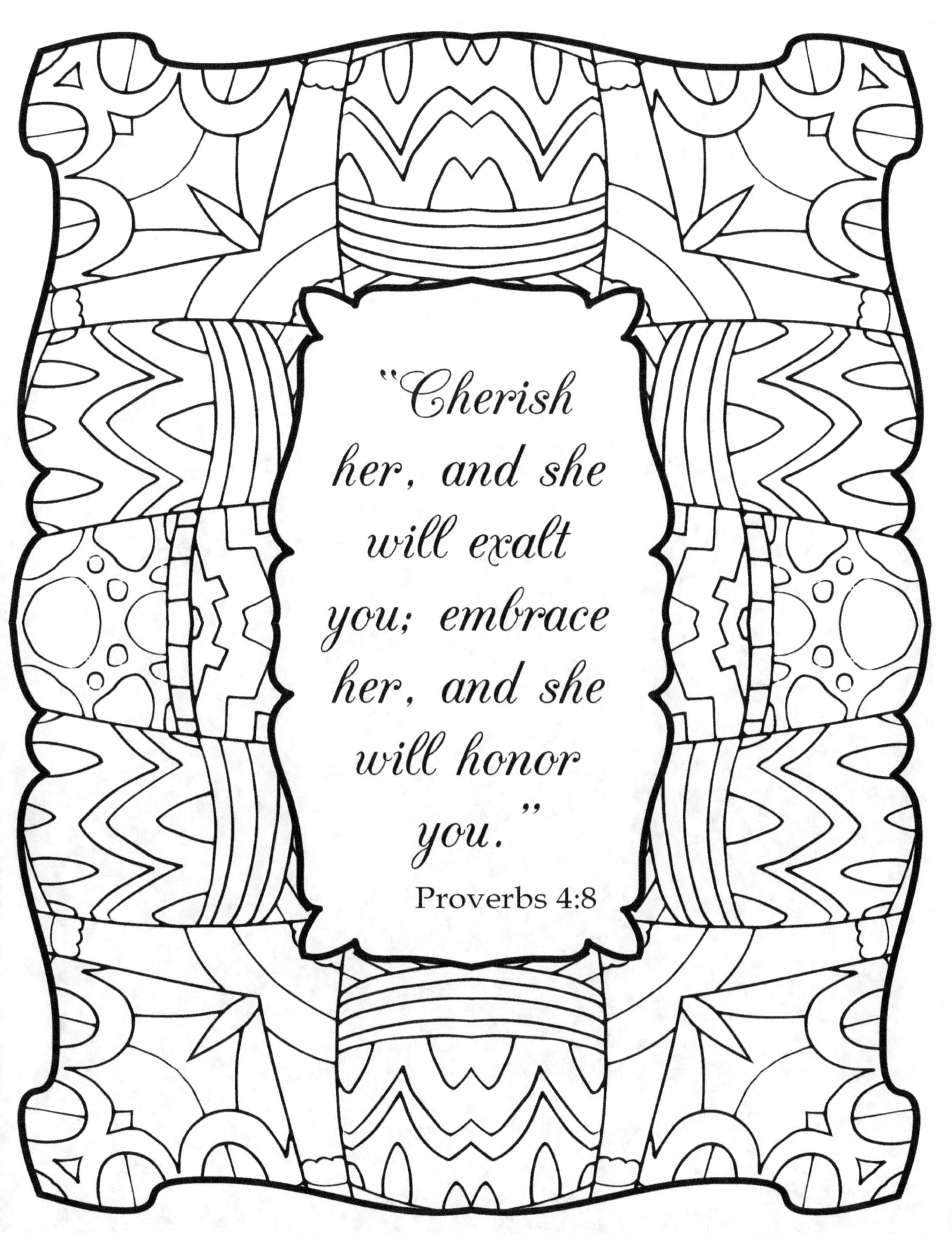

"Cherish her, and she will exalt you; embrace her, and she will honor you."

Proverbs 4:8

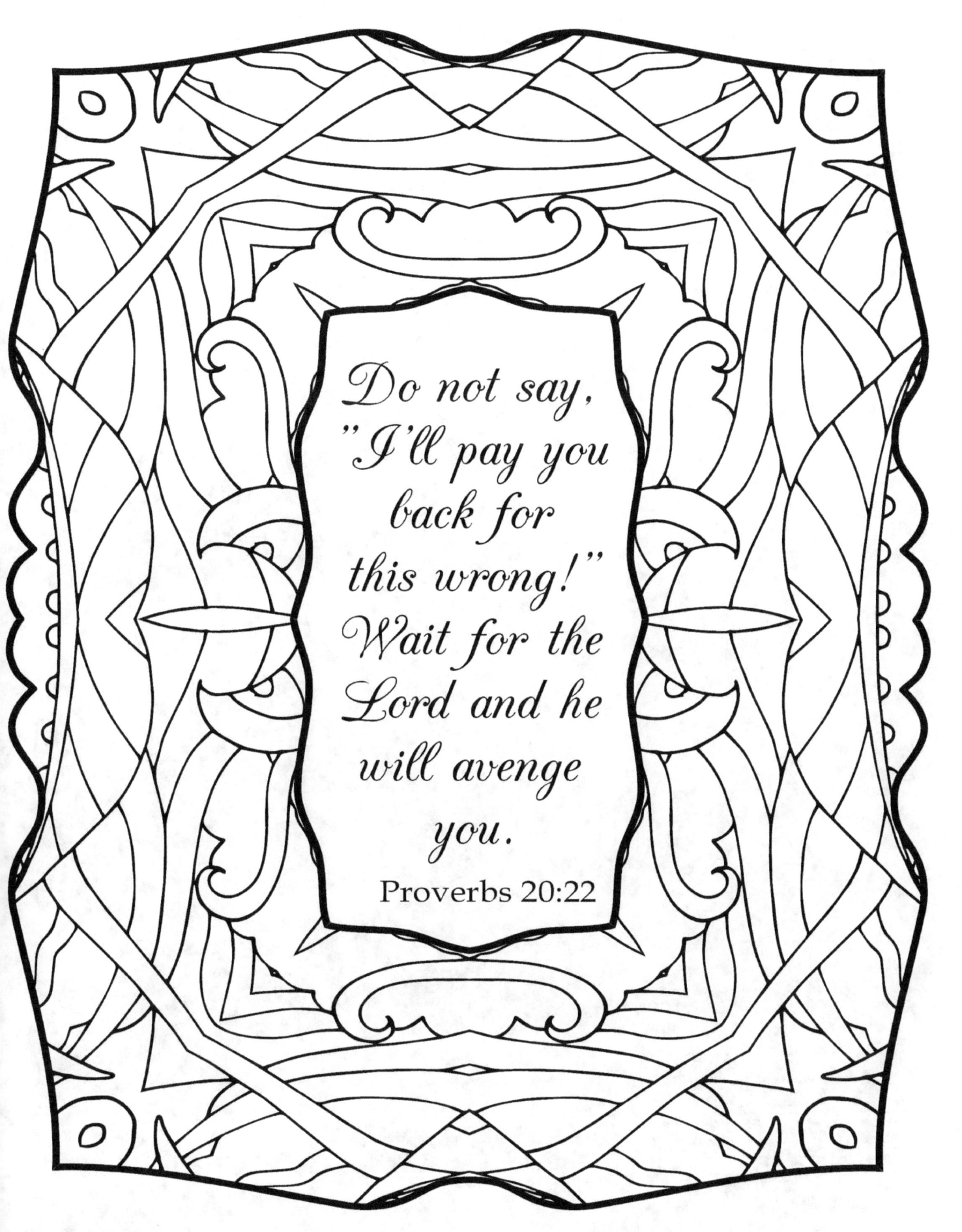

Do not say, "I'll pay you back for this wrong!" Wait for the Lord and he will avenge you.

Proverbs 20:22

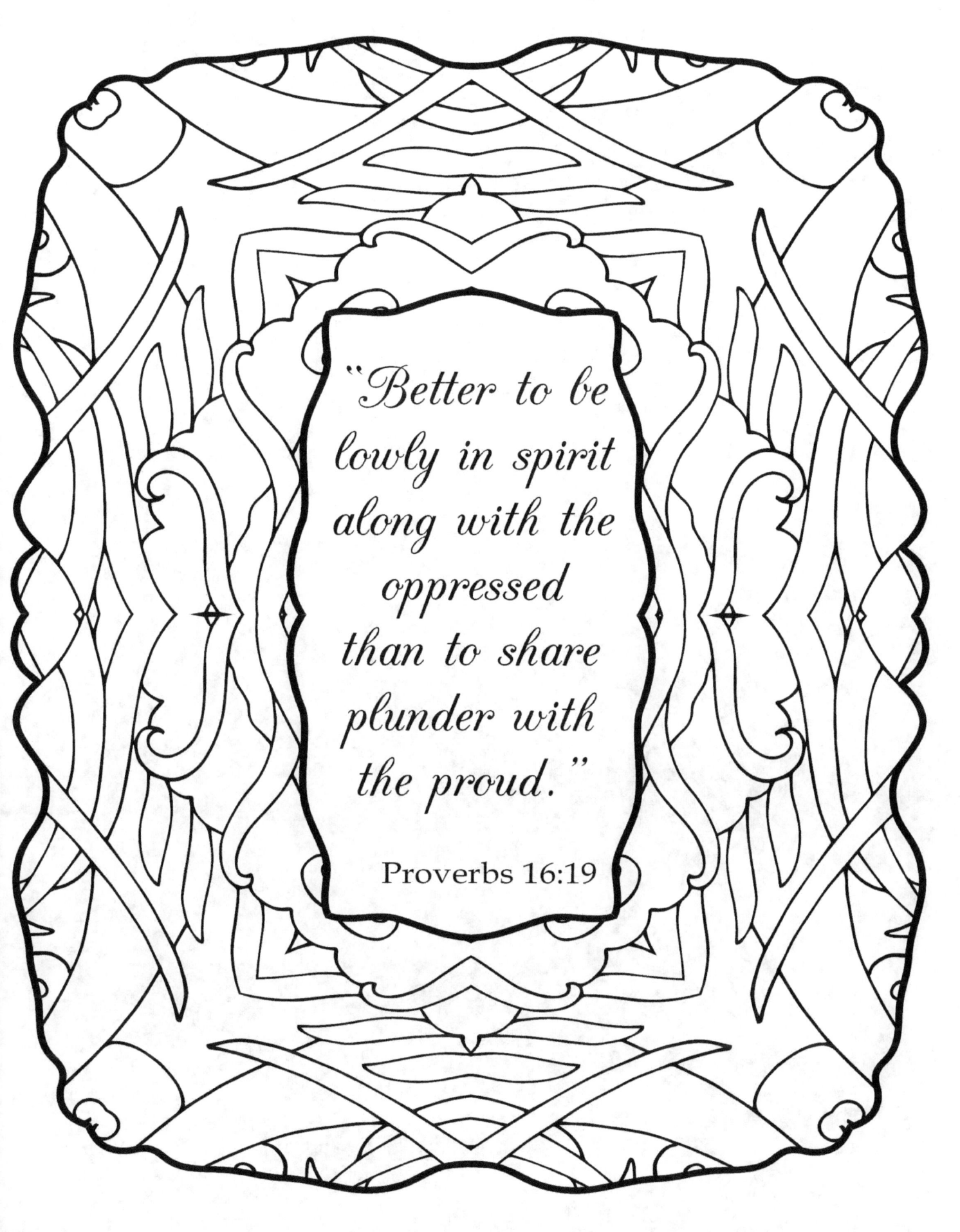

"Better to be lowly in spirit along with the oppressed than to share plunder with the proud."

Proverbs 16:19

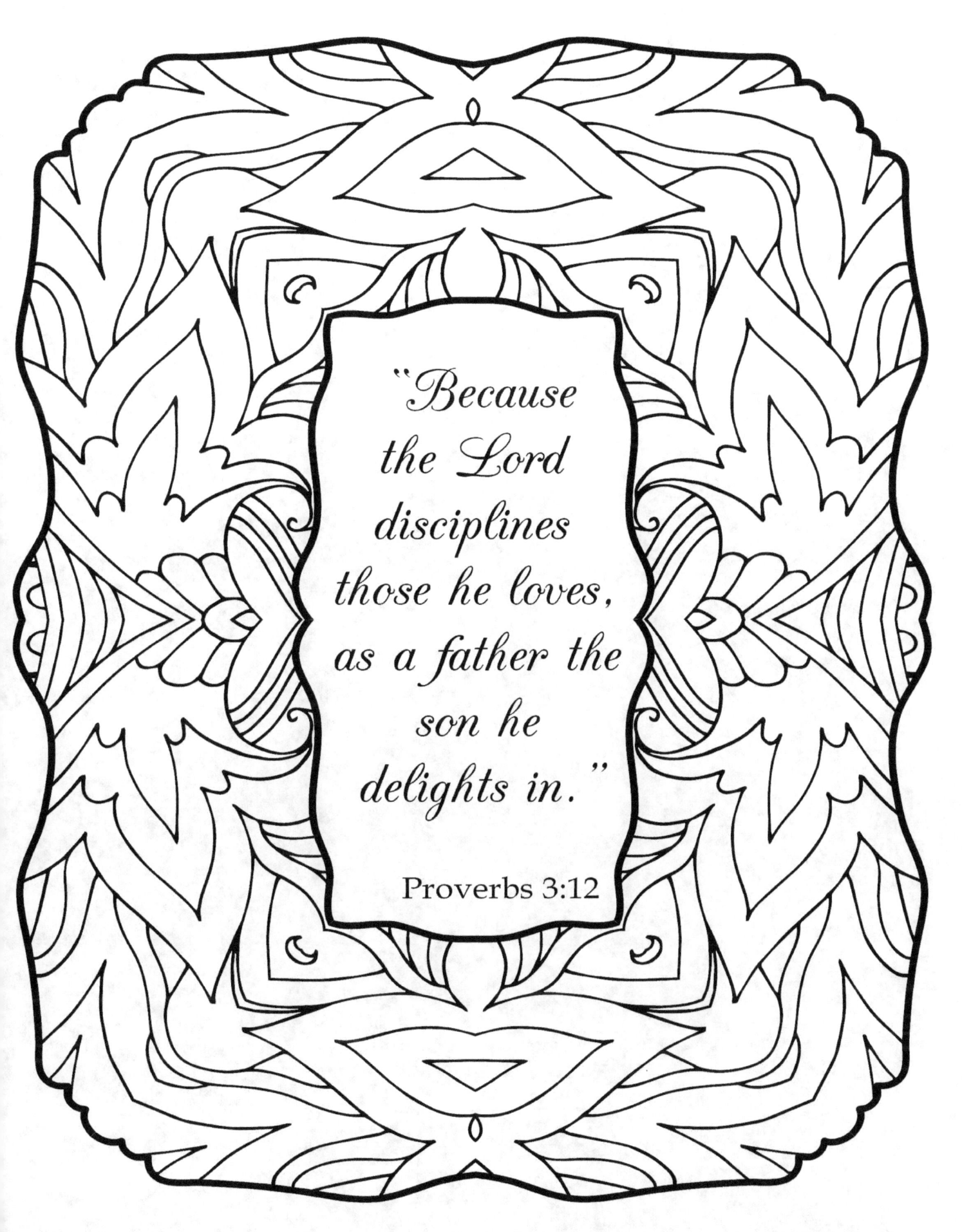

"Because the Lord disciplines those he loves, as a father the son he delights in."

Proverbs 3:12

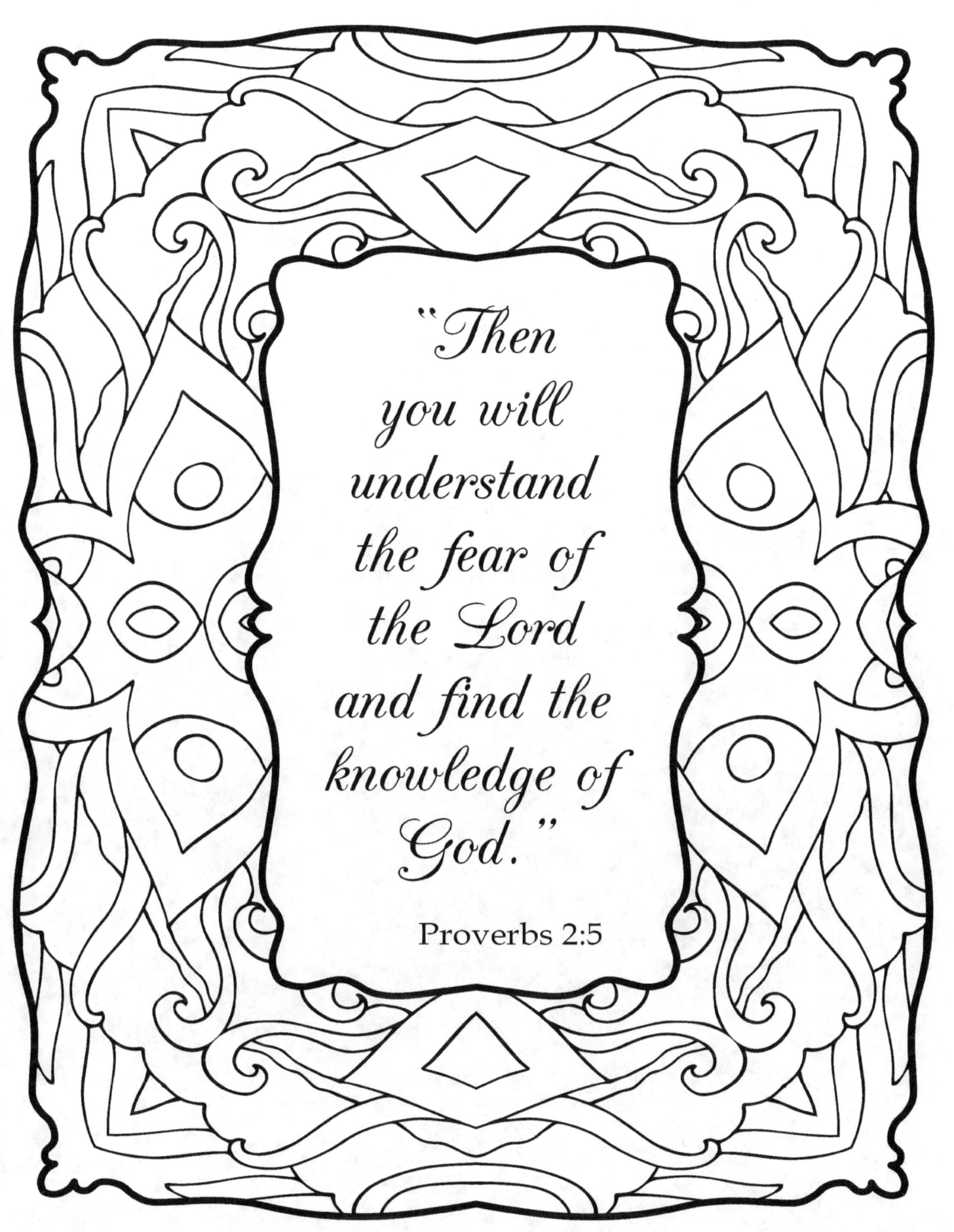

"Then you will understand the fear of the Lord and find the knowledge of God."

Proverbs 2:5

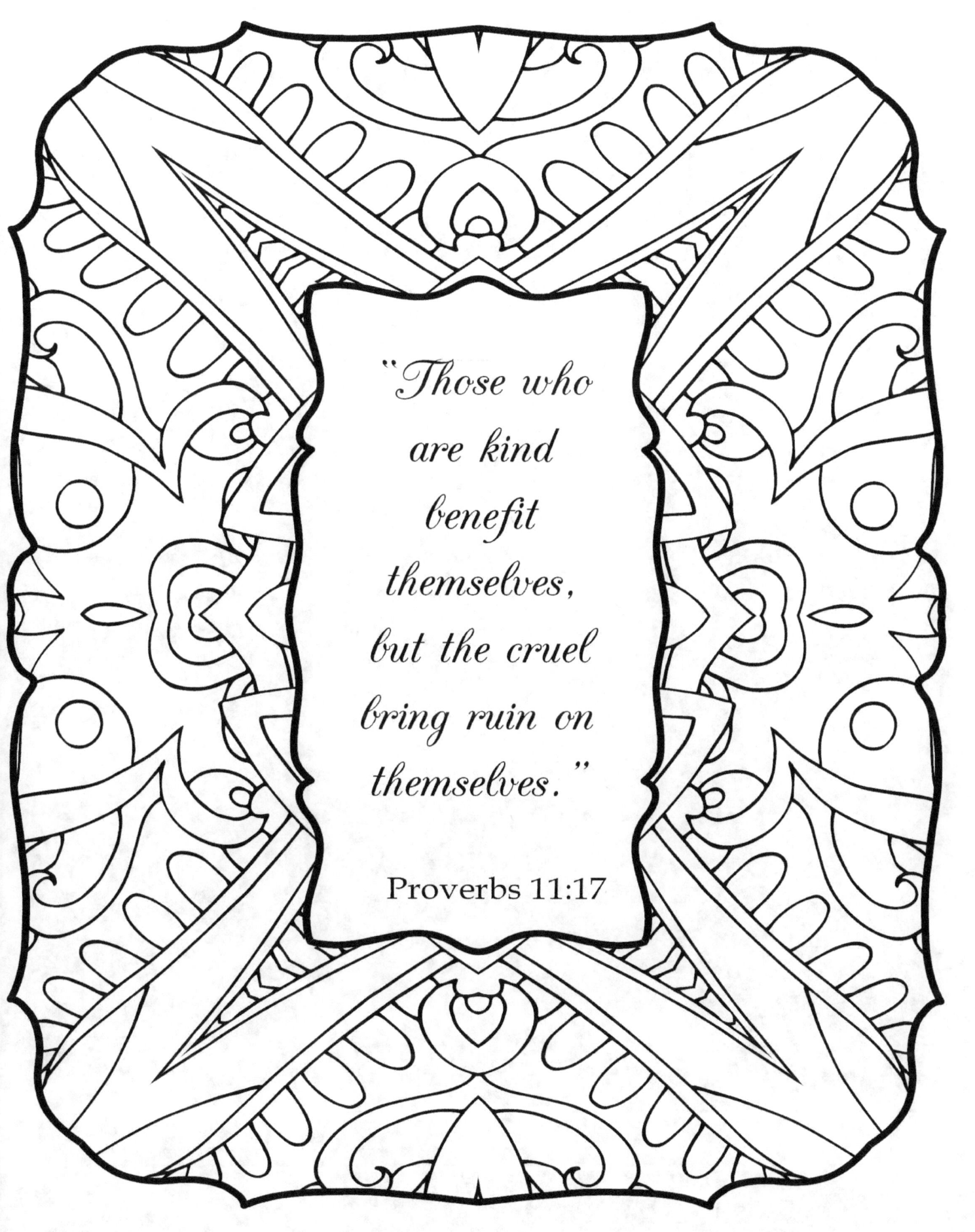

"Those who are kind benefit themselves, but the cruel bring ruin on themselves."

Proverbs 11:17

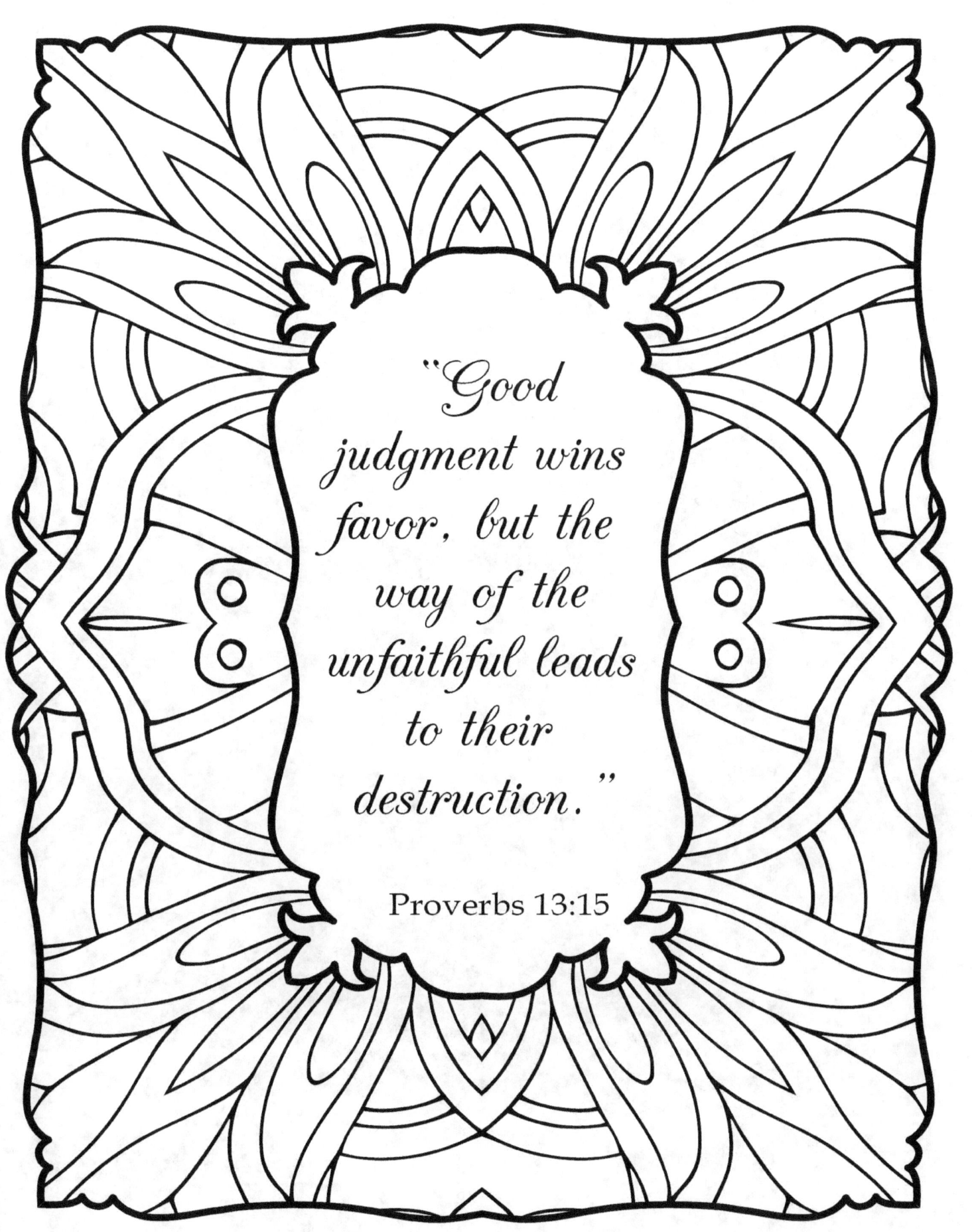

"Good judgment wins favor, but the way of the unfaithful leads to their destruction."

Proverbs 13:15

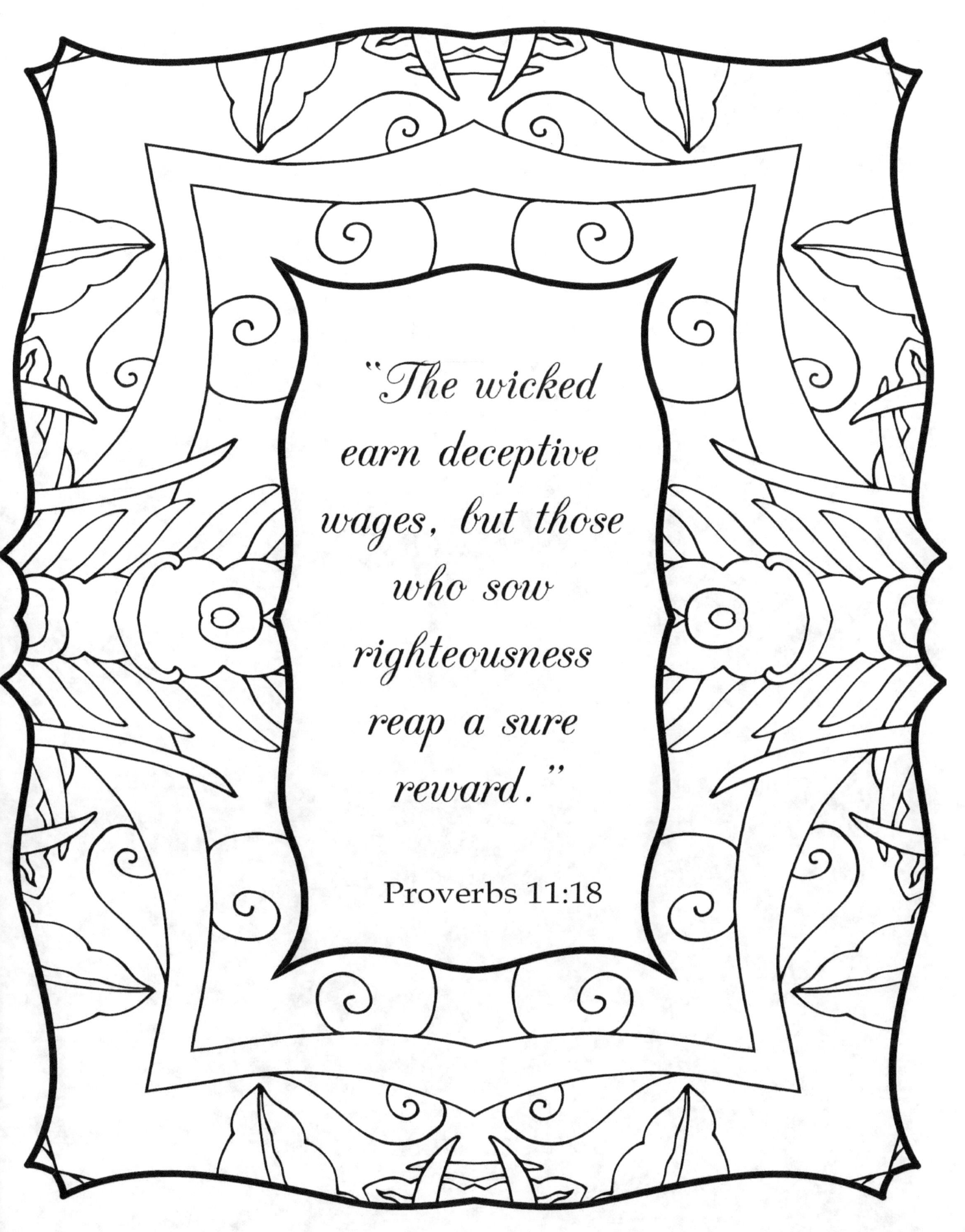

"The wicked earn deceptive wages, but those who sow righteousness reap a sure reward."

Proverbs 11:18

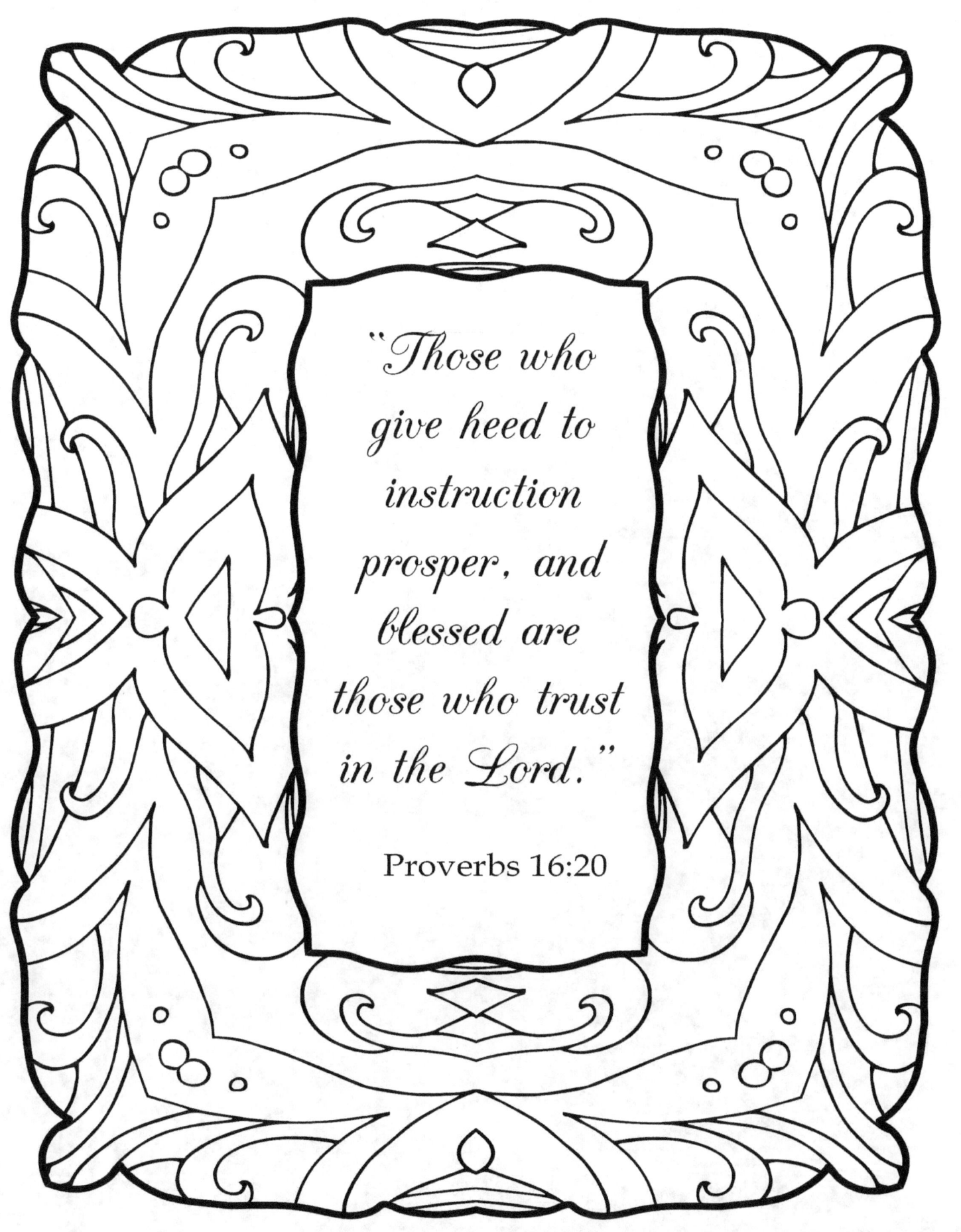

"Those who give heed to instruction prosper, and blessed are those who trust in the Lord."

Proverbs 16:20

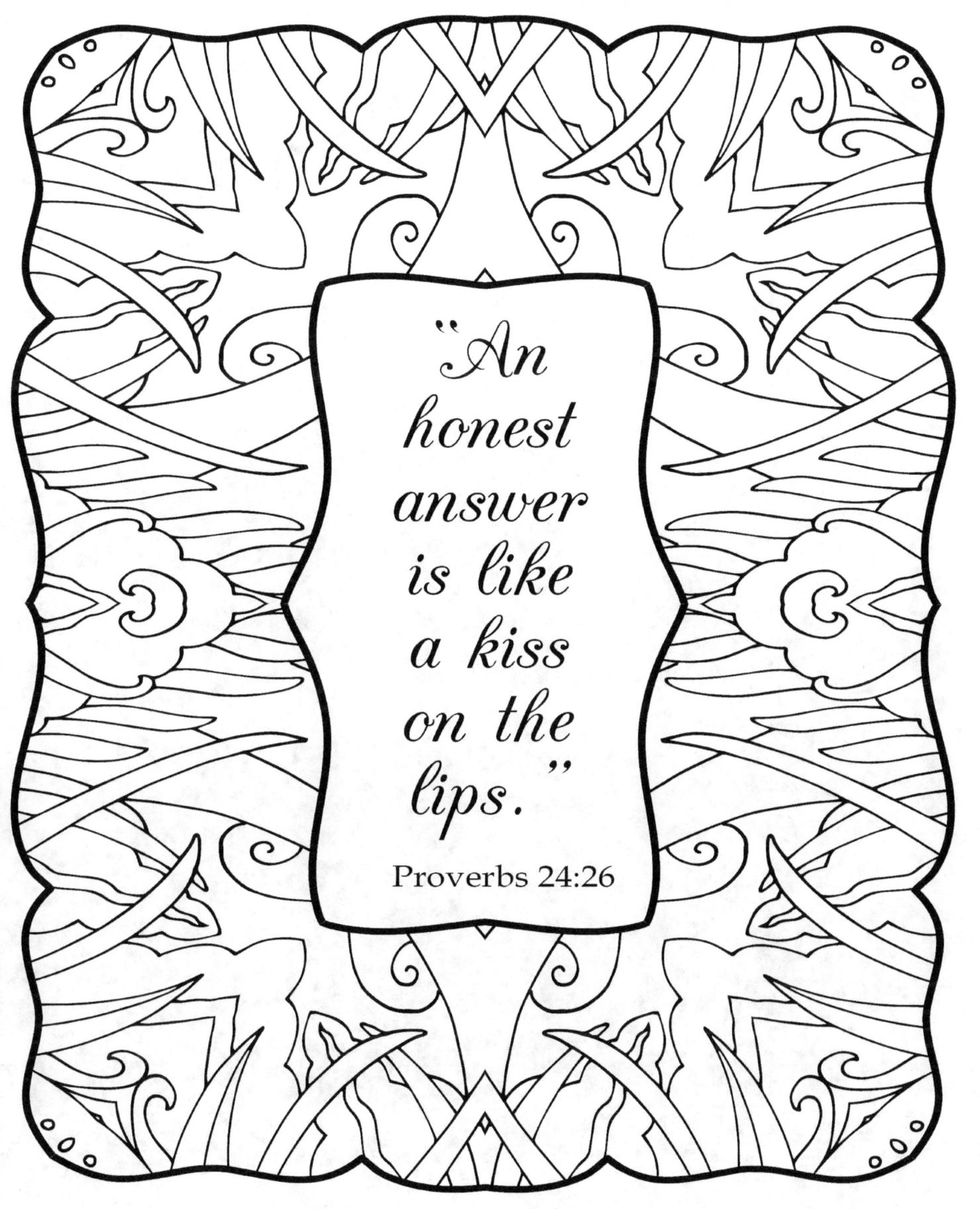

"An honest answer is like a kiss on the lips."

Proverbs 24:26

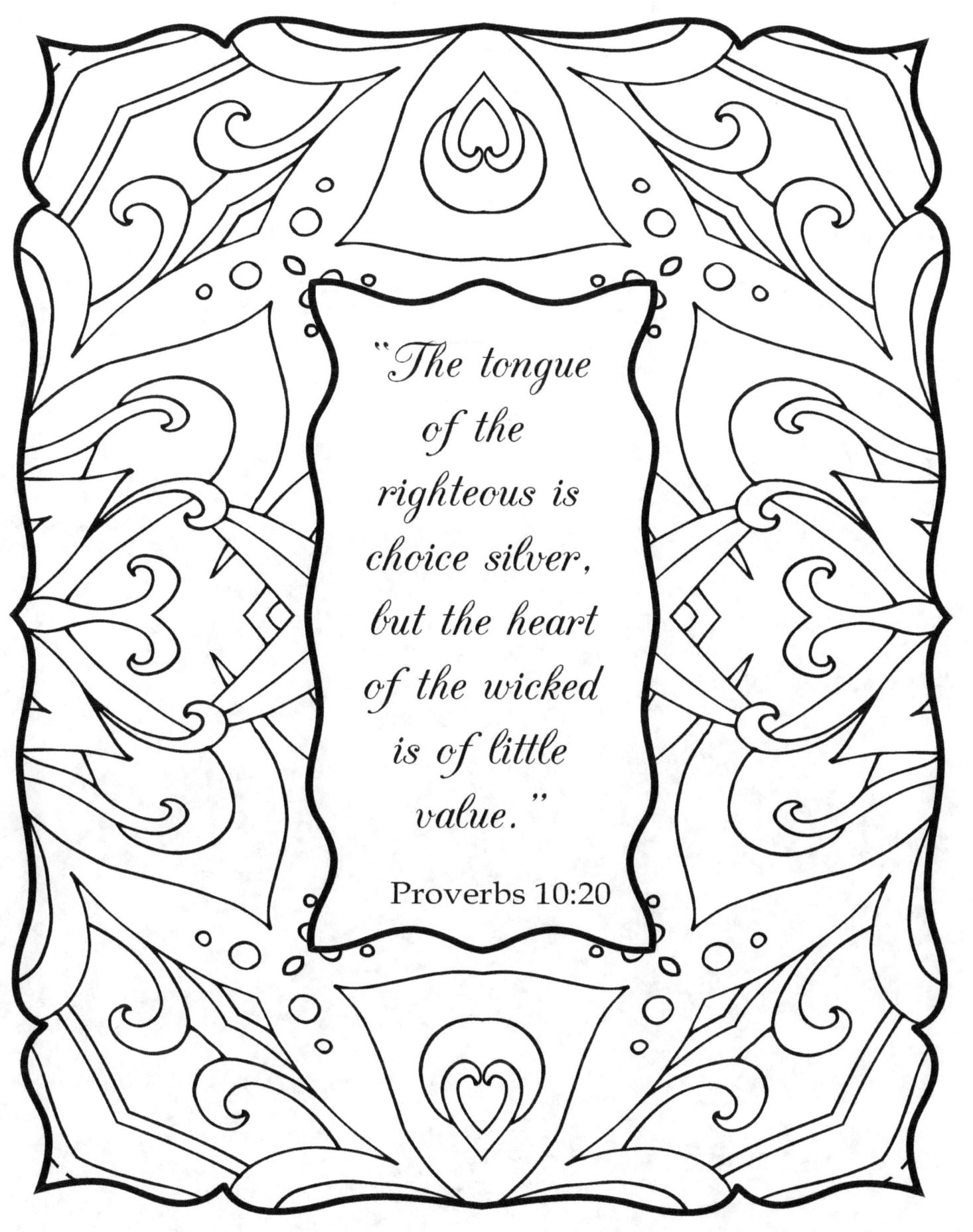

"The tongue of the righteous is choice silver, but the heart of the wicked is of little value."

Proverbs 10:20

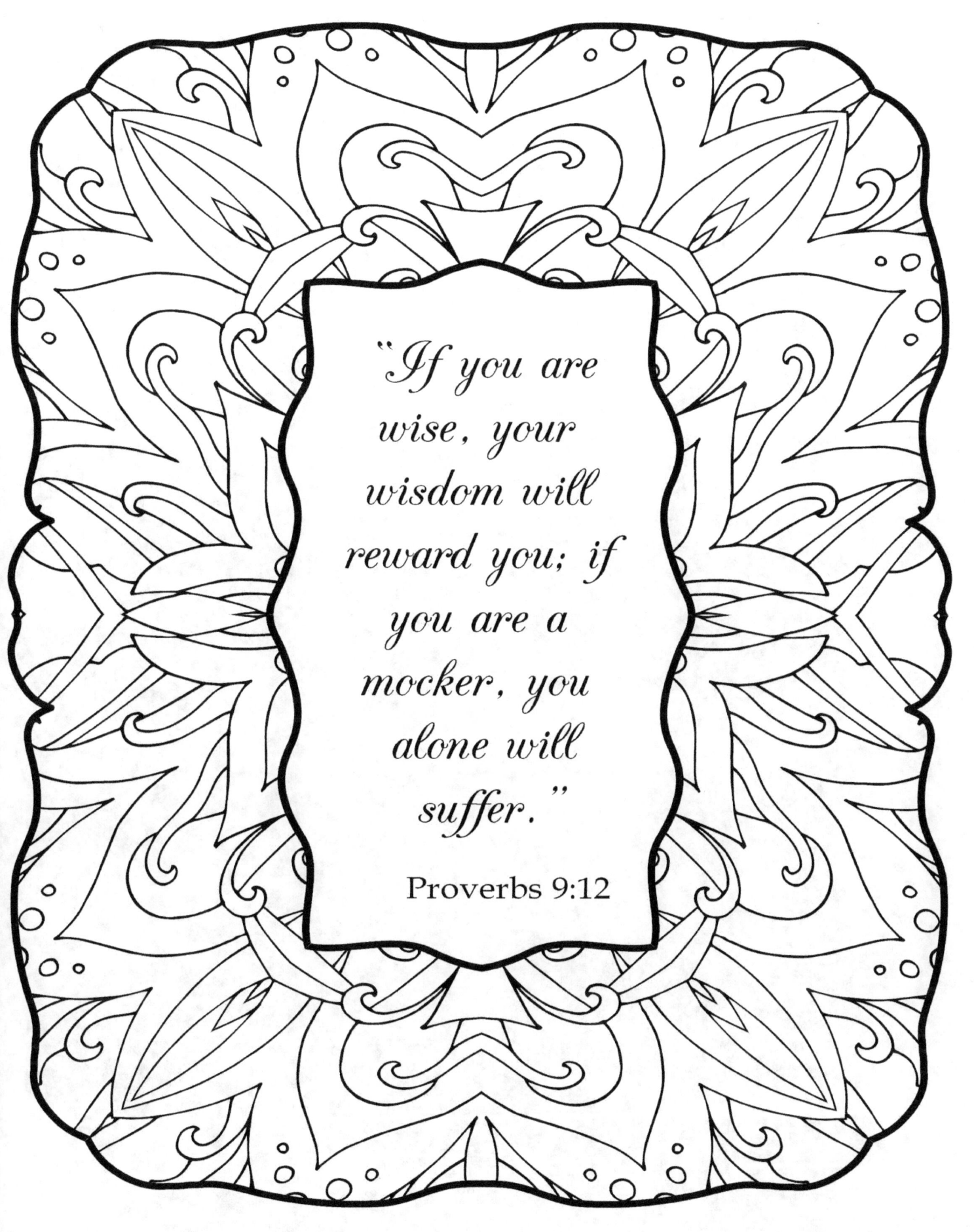

"If you are wise, your wisdom will reward you; if you are a mocker, you alone will suffer."

Proverbs 9:12

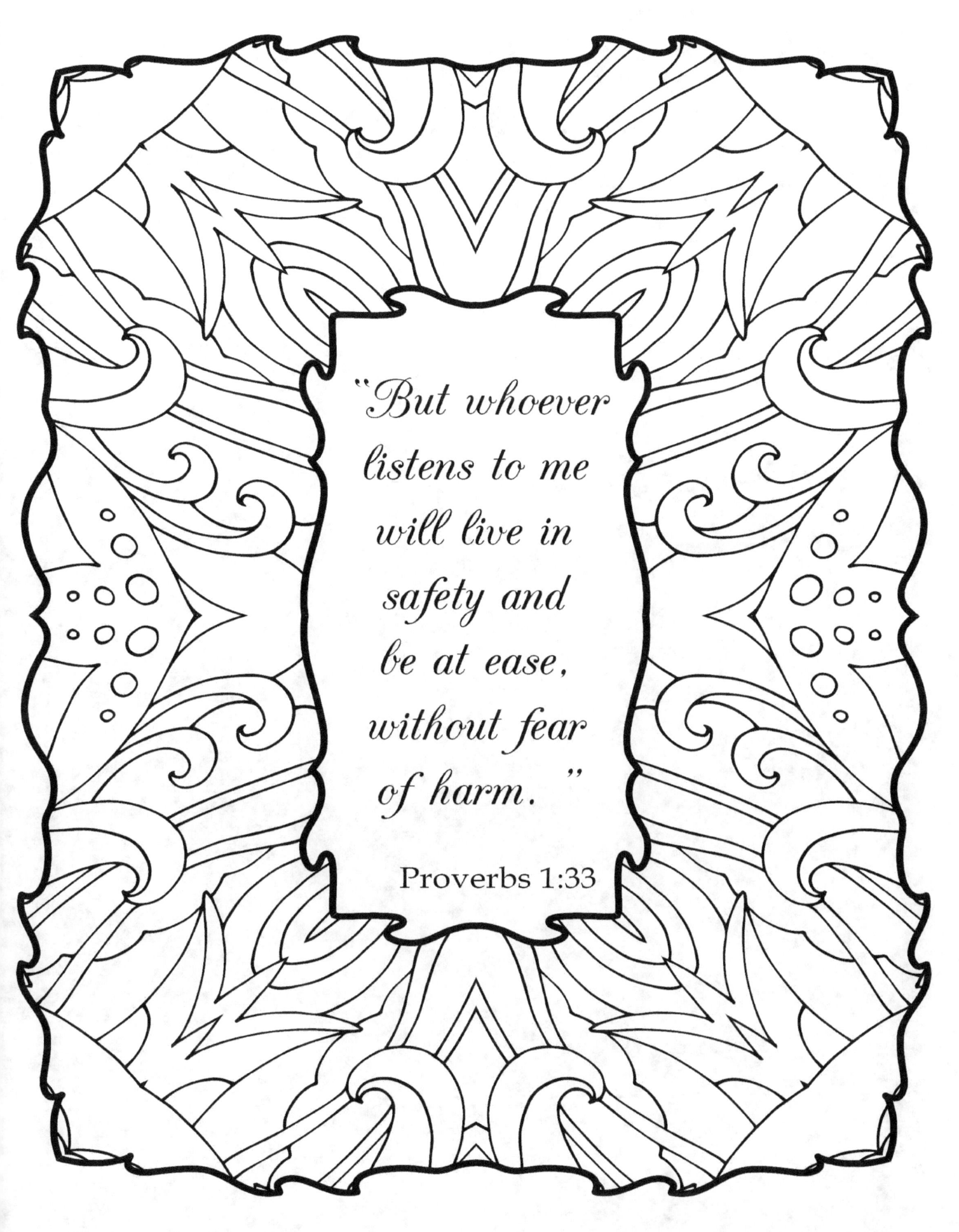

"But whoever listens to me will live in safety and be at ease, without fear of harm."

Proverbs 1:33

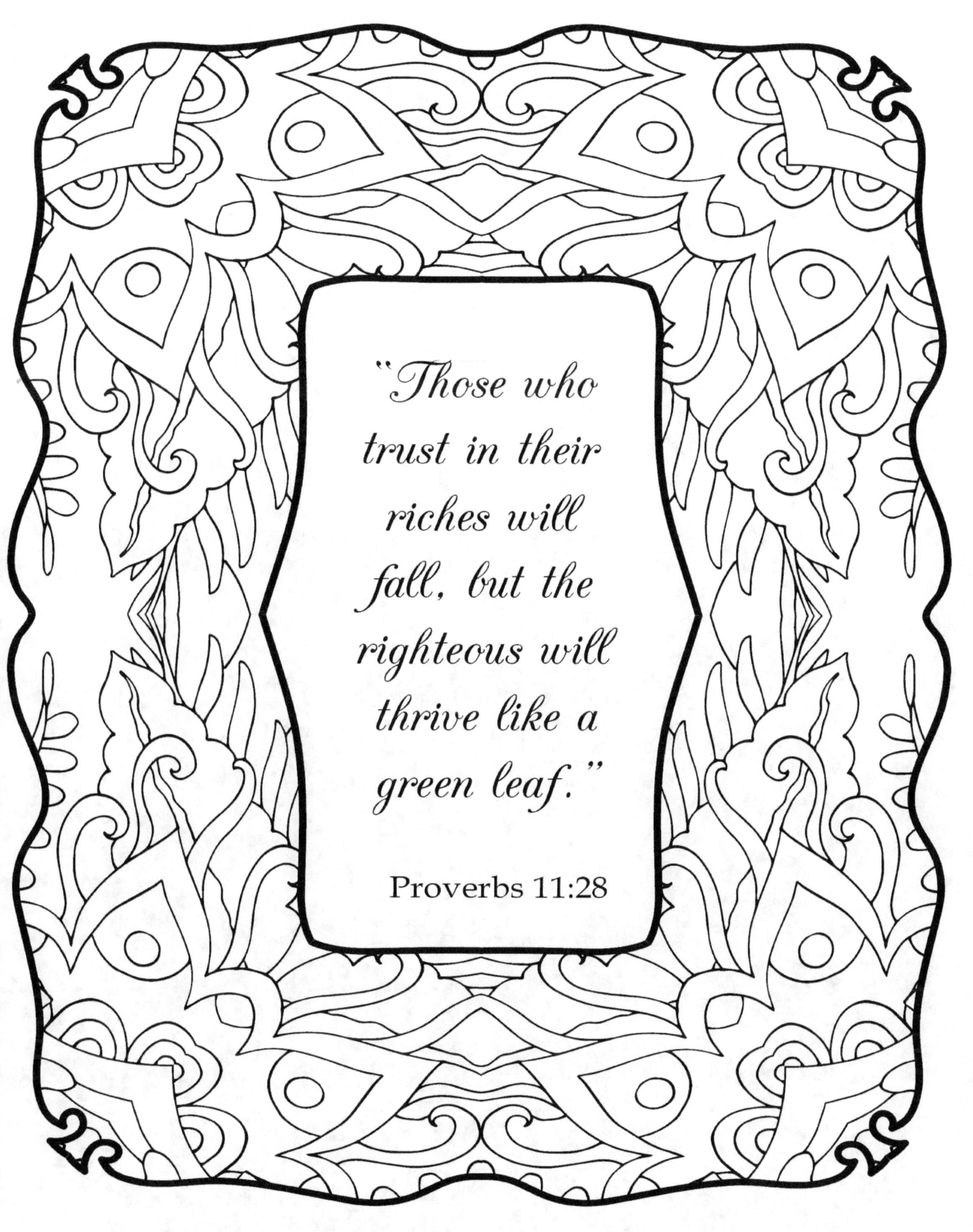

"Those who trust in their riches will fall, but the righteous will thrive like a green leaf."

Proverbs 11:28

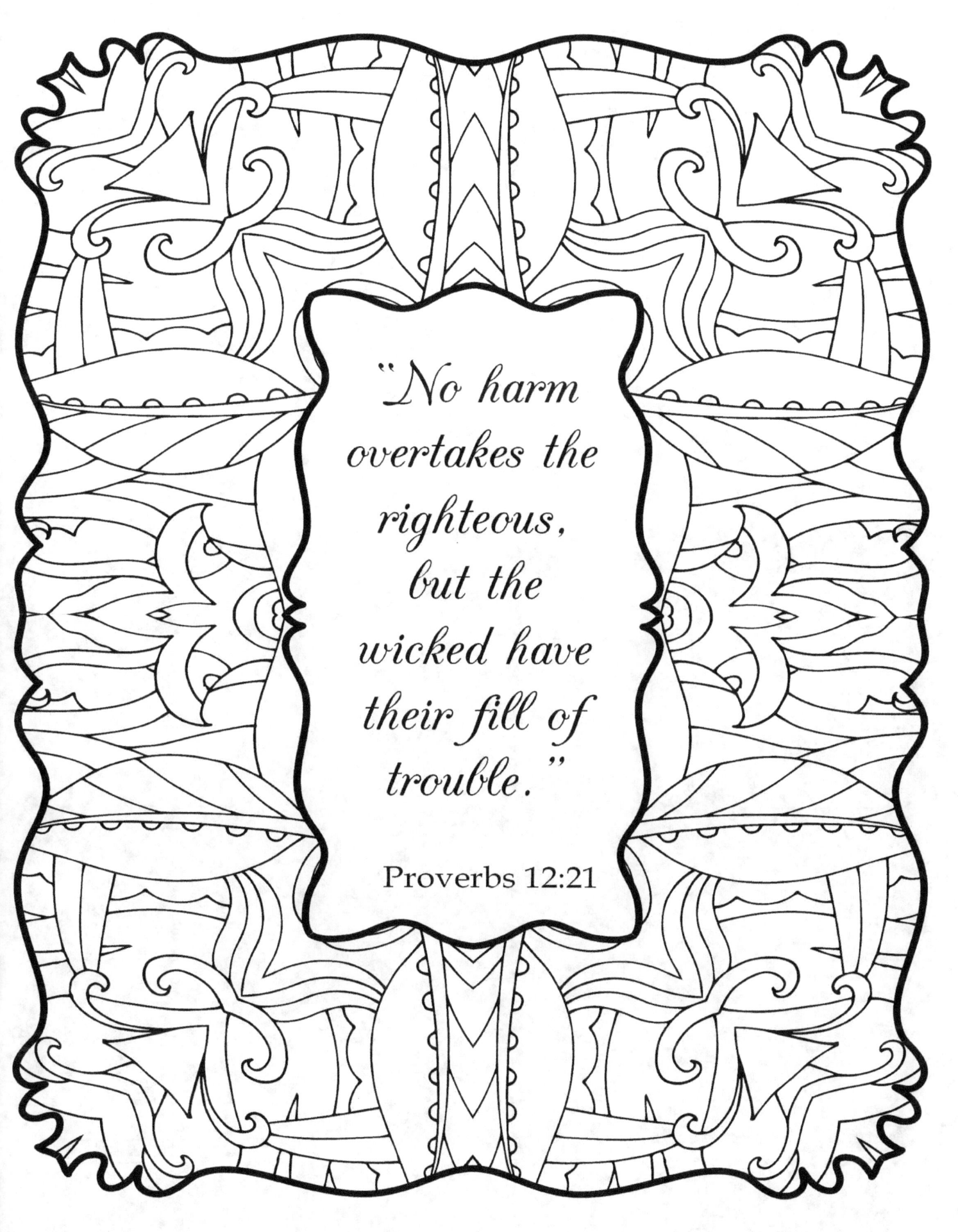

"No harm overtakes the righteous, but the wicked have their fill of trouble."

Proverbs 12:21

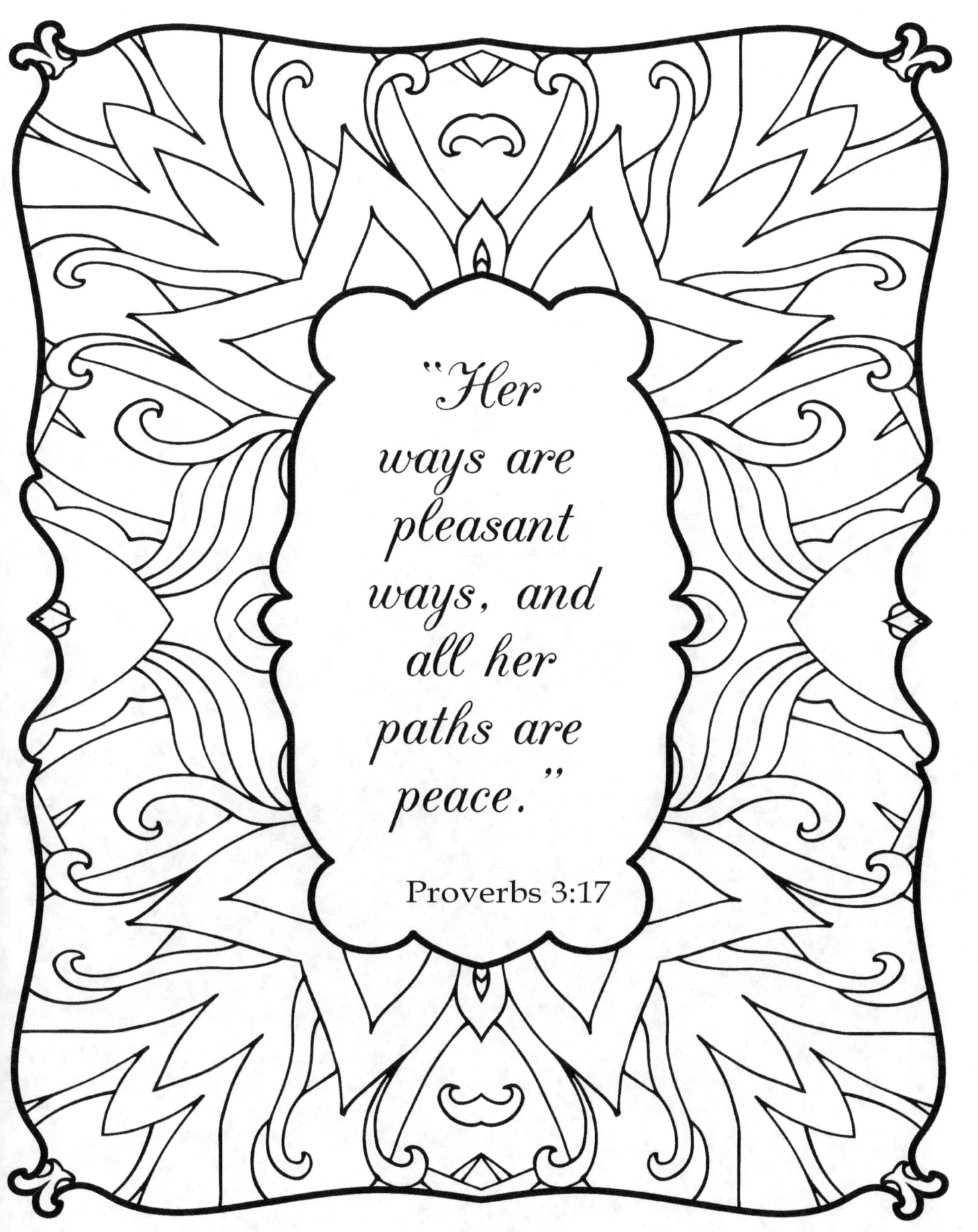

"Her ways are pleasant ways, and all her paths are peace."

Proverbs 3:17

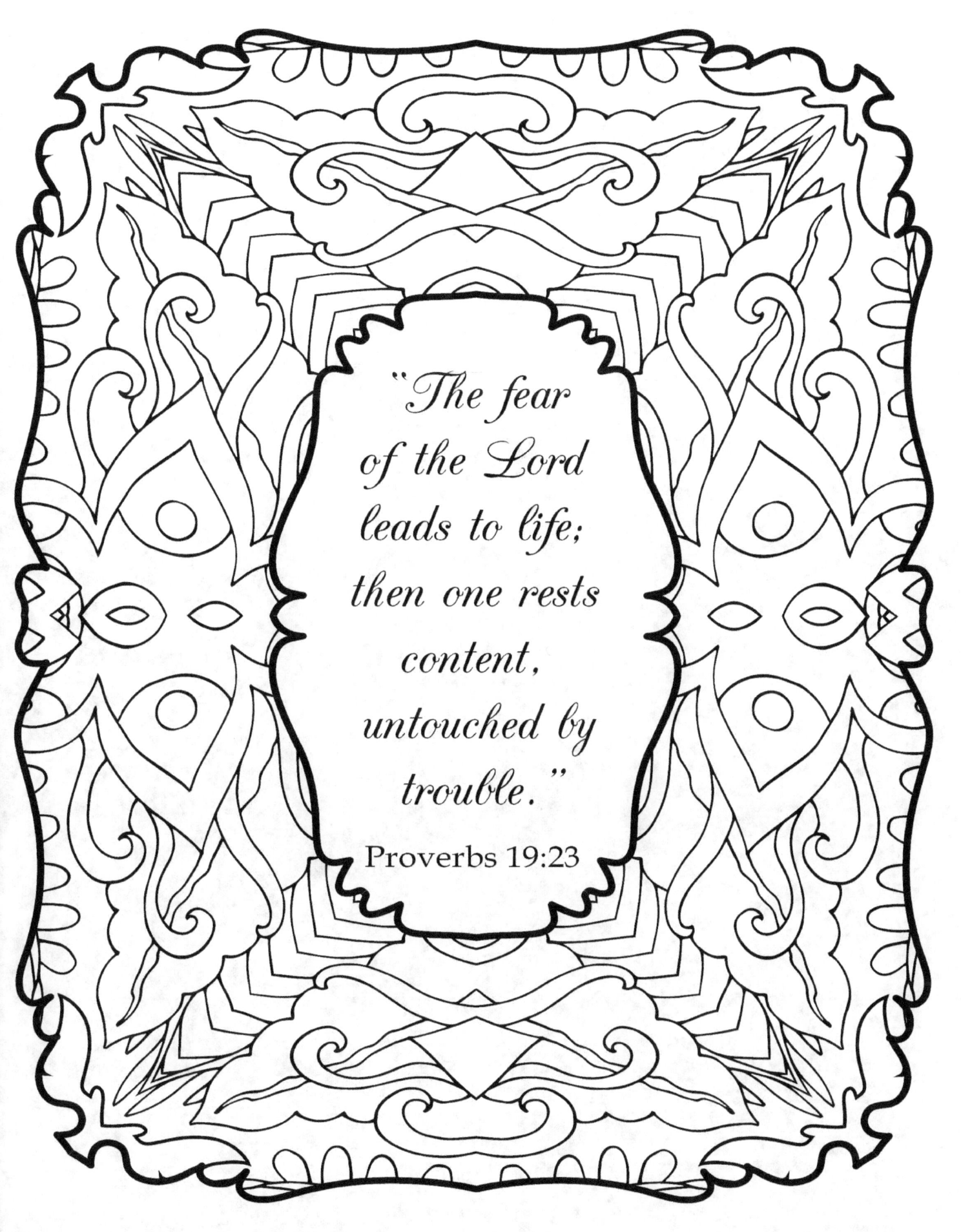

"The fear of the Lord leads to life; then one rests content, untouched by trouble."

Proverbs 19:23

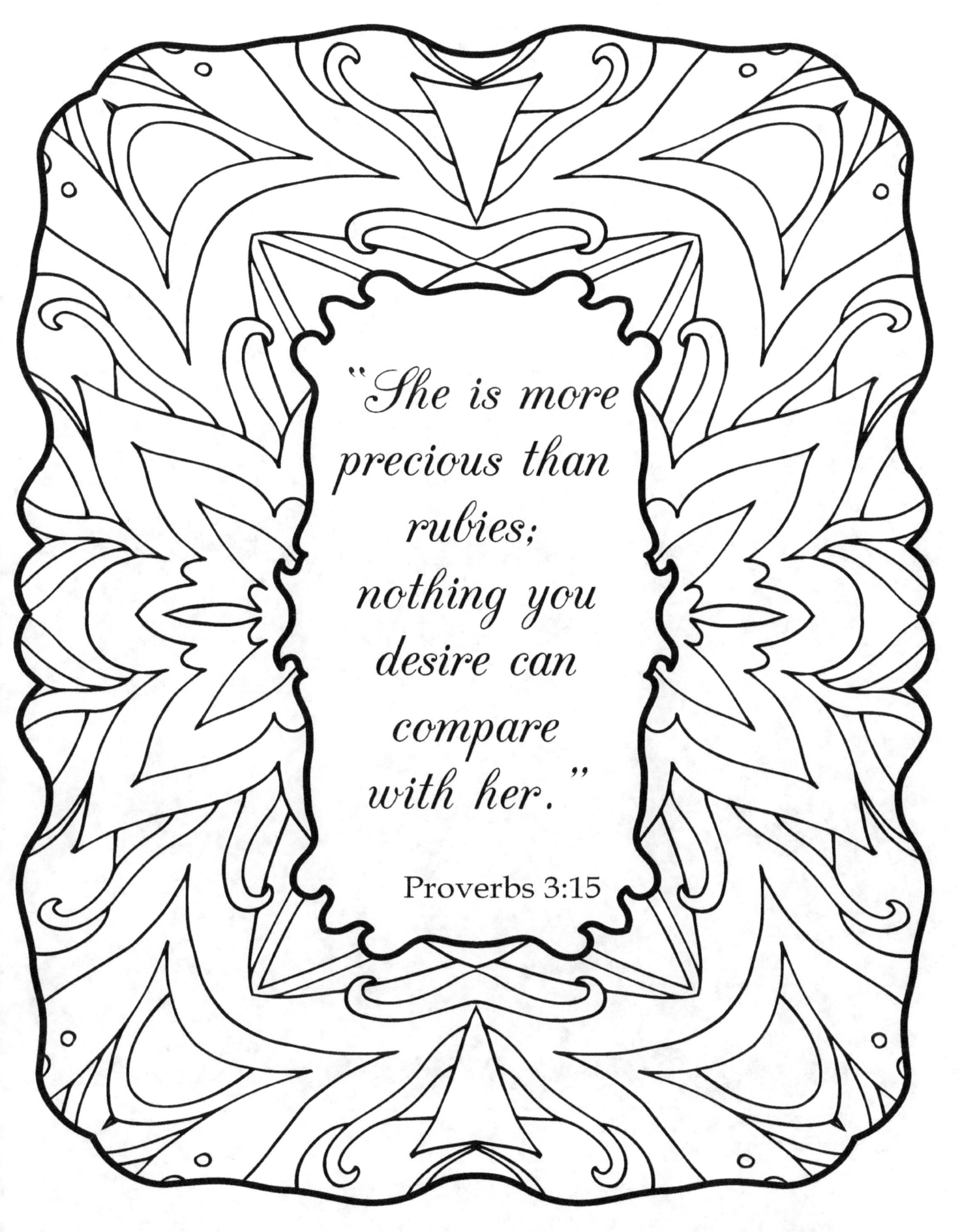

"She is more precious than rubies; nothing you desire can compare with her."

Proverbs 3:15

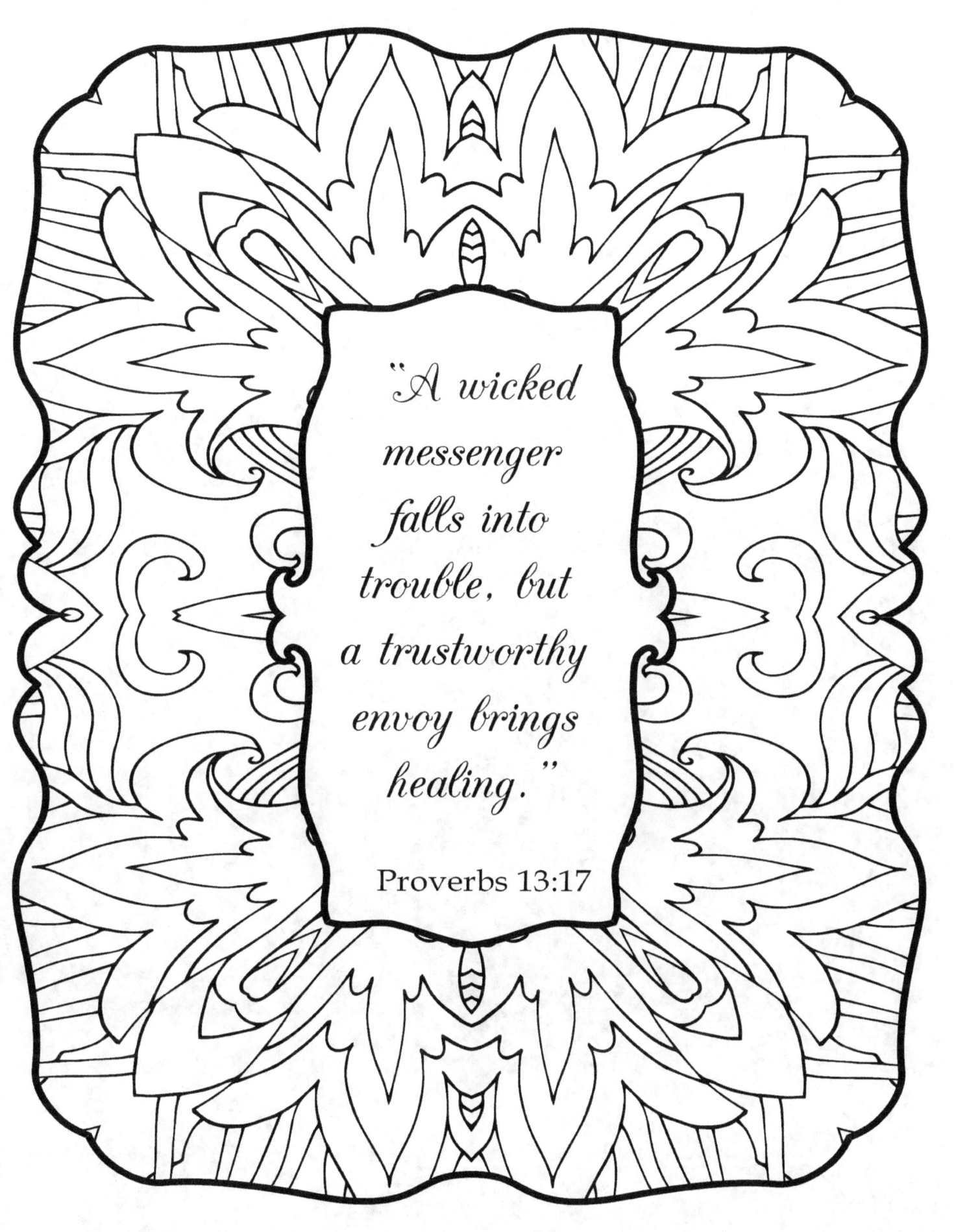

"A wicked messenger falls into trouble, but a trustworthy envoy brings healing."

Proverbs 13:17

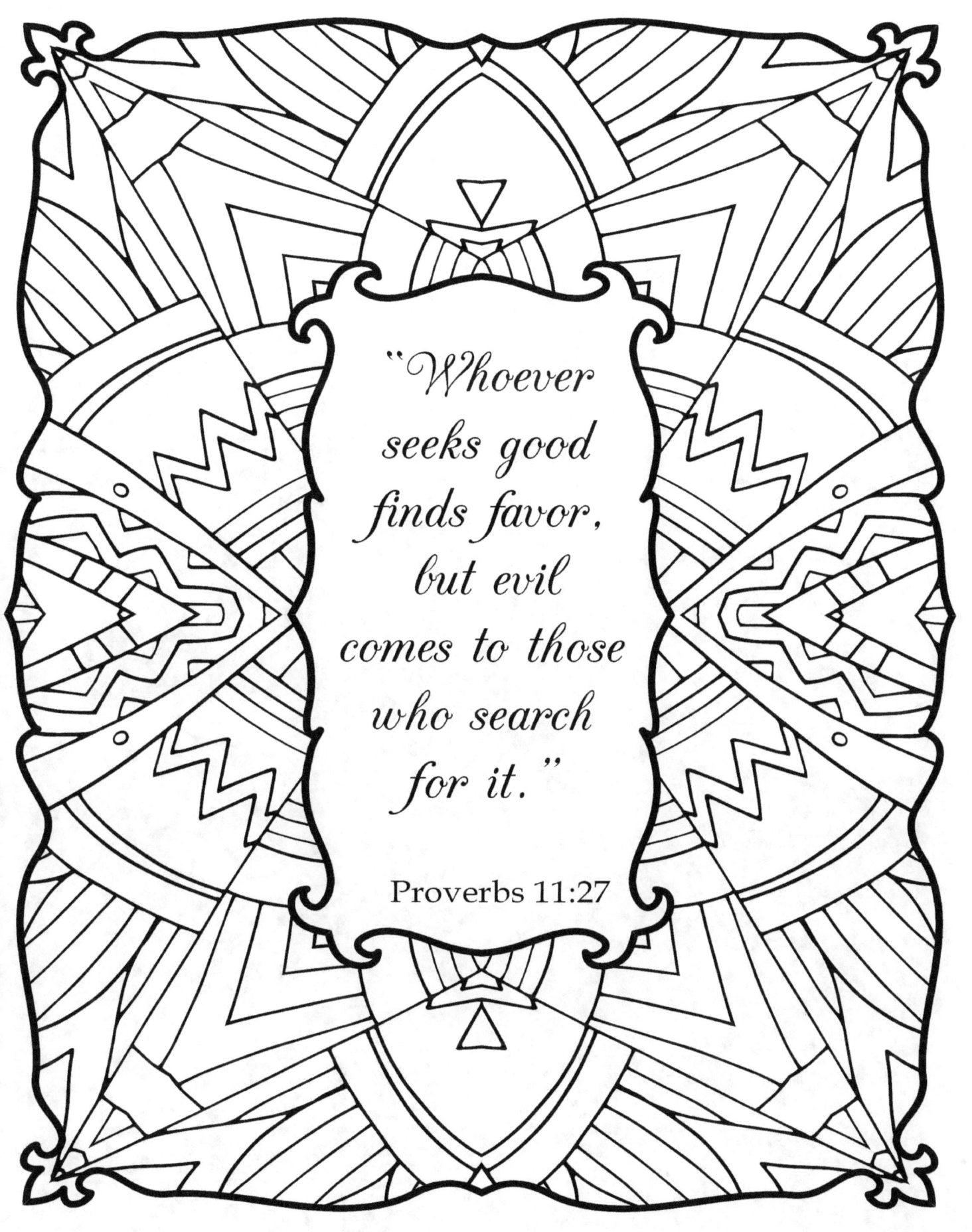

"Whoever seeks good finds favor, but evil comes to those who search for it."

Proverbs 11:27

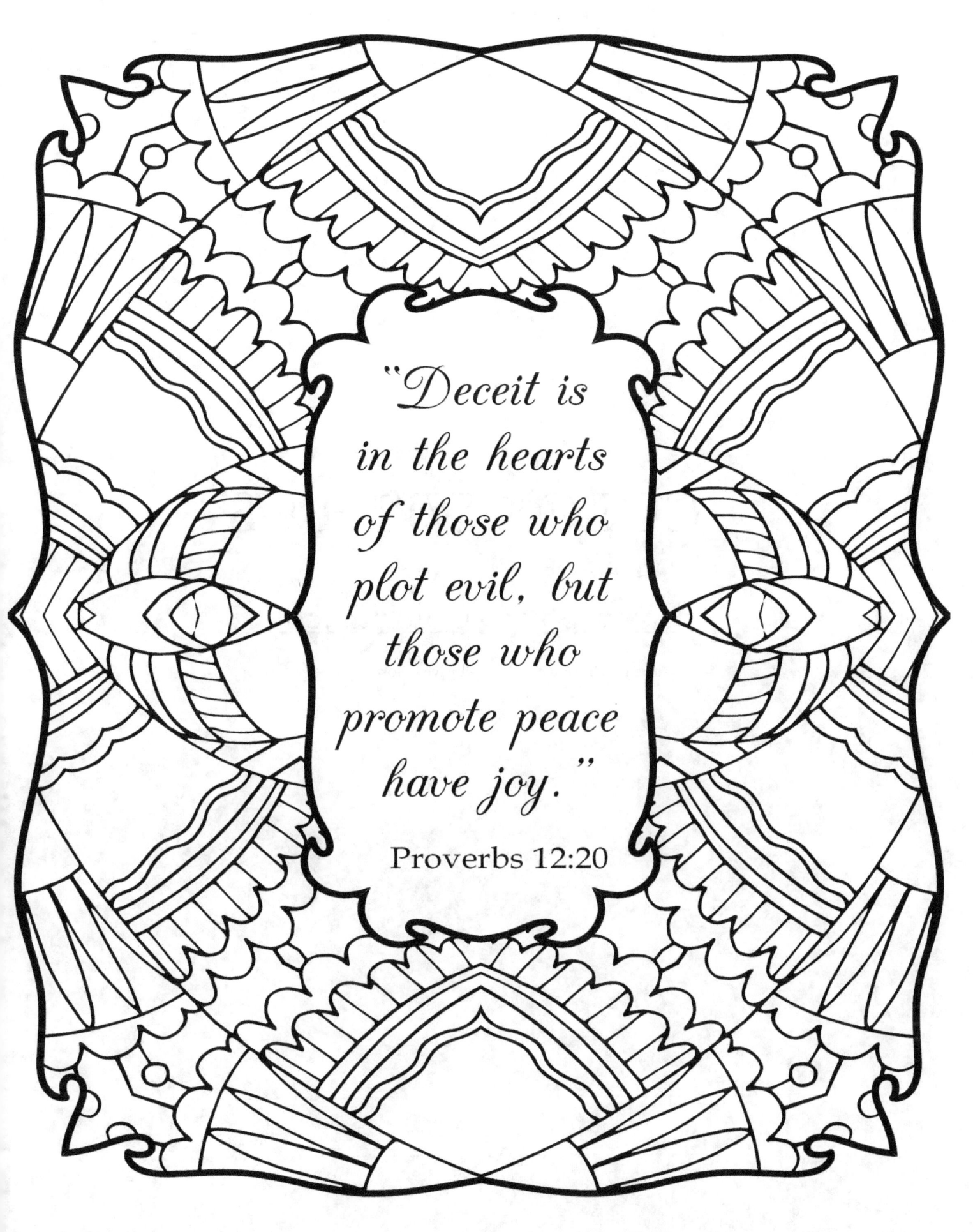

"Deceit is in the hearts of those who plot evil, but those who promote peace have joy."

Proverbs 12:20

COLOR WITH US

www.LovinkColoring.com

Visit our website for more exclusive coloring pages or books

www.ingramcontent.com/pod-product-compliance
Lightning Source LLC
Chambersburg PA
CBHW08082518O526
45168CB00006B/2575